The Prayers of Many *is a book* corporate prayer. *Each page conta* scripture to illustrate the dynamic a *praying. This is a book that describes the journey that Mike and his team have embarked on to make corporate prayer accessible to all in an atmosphere of joyful, worshipping church family life.*

STUART BELL
Senior Pastor – Alive Church, Lincoln

Mike has written a great resource which will not only inspire many to pray but gives practical tools for how we can sustain corporate prayer and once again place the prayer meeting as the engine room of the church. Biblical, passionate and humble, just like the author.

MIKE PILAVACHI
Soul Survivor

Mike sees corporate prayer as the engine room of church life, without it we fail. He brings great insight and practical instruction into how praying together produces a united army, passionate to see God's purposes succeed. It makes compelling reading and will be highly motivating material for every church to follow.

LIZ HOLDEN
New Ground Churches

As you read this book be ready to be inspired & provoked to the power of individual & corporate prayer. Jesus rebuked his disciples for not watching & praying with him for just an hour. We are living at a time when many Christians of this generation have exchanged the discipline & act of prayer with other programs. Matthew 26:40-41 "Watch & pray so that you will not fall into temptation". Let us never postpone prayers, because prayer works!

EDWARD BURIA
Kerith Church, Meru, Kenya

THE PRAYERS OF MANY

Published by Relational Mission

Jubilee Family Centre, Norwich Road, Aylsham, Norfolk, NR11 6JG, UK

www.relationalmission.com

ISBN   978-0-9954778-8-9

Acknowledgements

Scripture quotations are from the ESV® Bible (The Holy Bible, English Standard Version®), copyright © 2001 by Crossway, a publishing ministry of Good News Publishers.

Used by permission. All rights reserved.

A catalogue record of this book is available from the British Library

Cover Design by Daniel Goodman

Typeset in Adobe Garamond Pro

THE PRAYERS OF MANY

By Mike Betts

Published by *Relational Mission*

To Walter Long and Joan Gowing.

I owe much to their presence, passion and petition in prayer to God in my local church – it has, throughout my Christian life, not only taught me the utter necessity of corporate prayer but has modelled to me how to pray in such settings and inevitably has paved the way for much of the blessing in local church life that I have had the privilege to see.

And the best is still yet to be!

CONTENTS

FOREWORD

The surveys make sobering reading. There are clear signs that the church prayer meeting is declining and even dying in the majority of churches (less than half even hold one), at the very time our nation needs concerted, corporate intercession more than ever before.

Meanwhile, the Apostle Paul's clear injunction to the gathered church "that petitions, prayers, intercession and thanksgiving be made for… all those in authority, that we may live peaceful and quiet lives in all godliness and holiness" (1 Timothy 2:1-2) is routinely ignored. It may be the biblical commandment most commonly and unashamedly disobeyed by God's people in the UK today. We get the leaders we pray for, it seems. No wonder we struggle to live peaceful and quiet lives in all godliness and holiness!

Something within me, and within Mike Betts too, cries "Not on our watch!" The prayer meeting must not, it shall not, die on our watch. We must light beacons of intercession throughout the land. Certain places are catching fire! Over recent years it has become common for British churches to pray night-and-day – this was unthinkable twenty years ago. *Thy Kingdom Come* now gathers more than a million people from every Christian tradition to pray as one at Pentecost for the Spirit to come and for Christ's kingdom to come (which are arguably the same things). The Redeemed Christian Church of God gathers 40,000 people to pray all night at the Excel Centre in London. The *Enough* initiative, led by Mike, creates hubs of intercessory prayer throughout the land. There are many encouraging signs as God calls his church to rediscover the extraordinary power of concerted prayer once again in this generation.

This compelling volume explains why corporate prayer matters *biblically*, the difference it has made *historically*, and how to do it *practically,* using a series of helpful analogies (I was particularly pleased to see the chapter on family prayers, and the "Toolbox" section at the end).

Mike Betts writes with the heart of a seasoned pastor to equip and inspire others. There is an authority that flows from those whose experiences of answered prayer have been salted with the disappointments of unanswered prayer. Their faith is enriched with faithfulness. As I've got to know Mike I have discovered that he is that rarest of things: a western church leader who devotes more of his time to prayer than the platform, to friendship than function, to talking with God about others rather than talking about God with others.

The message of this book is urgently necessary, and it comes from the hand of a seasoned practitioner, from the clear mind of a thoughtful intercessor, and from the brave heart of a father in the faith.

PETE GREIG

Pete is one of the founding champions of the 24-7 Prayer movement and leads Emmaus Rd with his wife Sammy. They live in Guildford with their two sons, and their two dogs, Noodle & Crumble. Pete is an ambassador for the NGO Tearfund and served for seven years on the senior leadership team of HTB in London. Pete is a renowned author and his books include *Red Moon Rising*, *God on Mute* and *Dirty Glory*.

ACKNOWLEDGEMENTS

A few years ago I received some encouragement to the effect that writing books would be something that God would lead me into. It was also mentioned that, to give me confidence in this process, others would help, with the gifting they had, in the shaping of these books. That was true encouragement to me as I can tend towards self-doubt on whether I have anything to add to the large number of voices who already speak very eloquently on so many things! This is book number three and I can bear witness to the wonderful help I have had in writing *From the Inside Out, Relational Mission – a Way of Life* and this latest book *The Prayers of Many*. I do hope that, in this new book, my attempts to write simply on the matter of corporate prayer will mean that the material is well received and easily accessible for everyone. Most importantly that it will stir those who read it into action.

I especially want to thank Phil Whittall who, more than anyone, has helped me with editing and crafting the material into its present form. He has been and continues to be an enabler and facilitator to me in writing. He helps get onto paper the things stored within my heart; this is a precious help. Penny Taylor for her tireless servant heart, helping me in so many ways both with this book and with many other things. Then there are many others who have helped bring this book to completion. So a special thanks to Jennie Pollock, Poppy Balding, Daniel Goodman and James Taylor for their time and expertise.

Finally to those who contributed their stories to the book, showing how corporate prayer has worked for them. Many thanks.

1
REVOLUTION

A CALL FOR A REVOLUTION
IN CORPORATE PRAYER

We live in an instant age. We are constantly connected and instantly updated. If my phone doesn't start an app in a just a few seconds I wonder what's going wrong. We don't like waiting because we're busy people after all. Change (especially in other people) should happen quickly and so on and so on. The western world is not a very patient place. So when I use the word revolution, it can too easily conjure up the image of something that is happening very quickly. Yet even a brief (after all that may be all we have time for) look at the history books should tell us that revolutions happen over years not days, and certainly not hours, minutes or seconds. The French Revolution of the 18th century took twelve years. The American Revolution lasted eighteen. The Industrial

Revolution was as long as eighty years! Revolution that brings about a lasting and significant change can take years of investment and sacrifice.

All of which must seem quite a dramatic start for a book about prayer. But I am convinced that when it comes to corporate prayer – the act of the church praying together – what we need is a nothing short of a revolution.

There are many great books on prayer from many great heroes of the faith. However, most of them have their focus on the individual and often have in mind the individual praying alone. Not much has been written about corporate prayer (although I think that is starting to change), and yet when it comes to prayer the Bible has much to say about praying together.

In 2013 I was listening to Pete Greig speak to a group of leaders I had gathered together. Pete is one of those guys I just mentioned – a hero of the faith who has written several great books on prayer. But Pete also knows a thing or two about corporate prayer. He has after all started a genuine prayer movement known as 24/7 Prayer that has been going for over twenty years now. As Pete was talking, he said:

Corporate worship in church life has been changed beyond recognition in the past 30 years through much energy and creativity. Imagine what corporate prayer in church life would look like now if the same attention had been given to that.[1]

I was so impacted by this statement. I could not stop thinking about it. I still haven't. So much so that I decided that as far as it depended on me, I would try to become part of the solution and not remain part of the problem. I was a worship leader in my early days as a leader and I can recall the dramatic and exciting exploration of corporate worship. It fuelled my imagination that such a journey with corporate prayer might also be possible.

Not only do we live in an impatient age, we live in an individual age. Individualism is a cultural preference where the desires of an individual are favoured over the collective needs. It pushes people towards self-reliance and independence. This affects people's spiritual growth and so we see much focus on

---

[1] Pete Greig, 'Forum 2013' – transcribed from *Relational Mission* recording.

self-help, self-improvement and personal development. This is as true inside the church as outside of it. For all the good it may do, it's not without its blind spots, weaknesses and dangers.

On paying closer attention to the teaching of the New Testament including those parts concerning prayer we see that it has a corporate context in mind. If you more easily think "how does this apply to me?" and not "how does this apply to *us*?" then you are thinking individually not corporately. If that happens a lot then we are in danger of losing vital aspects of biblical practice surrounding prayer. We need to strengthen our ideas about the very identity and nature of the church as the family, the people, the temple, the nation of God. The Bible anticipates that most of our Christian life will inevitably be worked out and filled out in a corporate context. With this in mind, mature, corporate prayer, specifically in the life of God's people, becomes something to prize and pursue.

As I reflect on my Christian life, many of the most significant events that I can recall are those that had corporate prayer at their core. In my early years as a Christian, the prayer meeting in my local church was the engine room of all that

God did. For many years the UK churches in what was known at the time as Newfrontiers, gathered three times a year for two days of prayer and fasting. I am convinced this was the engine room for all the remarkable things we saw God do over several decades. I remain convinced that when God's people pray it unleashes the resources of heaven upon earth in ways simply nothing else can do.

So how can we as churches living in an impatient and individualistic world invest in this revolution of prayer together?

GOING UP A DISTANCE

I was privileged to see the Olympic and World champion Mo Farah run his last middle-distance race. After this race he was going up a distance, into marathon racing. To do this he changed his routines, his training, his perspective and his goals. Even his middle-distance identity was something he was keen to redefine for the future journey ahead. It made me think that the church in the West needs to go 'up a distance' on corporate prayer. Our brothers and sisters in the Global South and East are far more able and well-trained than us in corporate prayer and we need to humbly learn from them. We need to apply ourselves to changing our dynamic of prayer in just the same diligent and sustained way Mo Farah applied himself to changing his running distance.

There are several important steps to take. Firstly, we need to rescue prayer from being a department or specialism. Too often prayer and intercession has come to be seen as a gift that only some people have. You know, those very proficient praying people who seem to thrive in prayer meetings, the ones people talk about as "intercessors" or "prayer warriors".

There is no gift of an intercessor in the Bible. There is however an activity of intercession which is for the whole church to engage in. Prayer is part of the inheritance of all believers – praying together is how we should live as believers.

In the family of churches that I lead we have begun over the past few years to invest in praying together, not just as a church but as groups of churches. Three times a year we would gather as many people as possible to pray on the same night, for the same things.[2] To engage as many people as possible we deliberately set the bar at a height everyone can jump over. We have worked hard to make it easy for anyone who follows Christ to come along and feel engaged enjoyment in praying together with others.

It's not news to say that the Church in the West is struggling. There is a pulse, but in many places it's a pretty weak one. A lot has been and will be said into investigating the cause of the problem and in proposing solutions to restore the patient to health. I, like many others, read the book of Acts to see what we can learn from how the apostles and the early church got things started.

The apostles, faced with exponential growth, still remained convinced that they should "give [their] attention to prayer and the ministry of the word".[3] The apostles had an awareness of the effectiveness of these key components and the utterly

---

[2] We called these prayer gatherings 'Enough' to state both that God is enough for us and that there are issues and injustices in our world that we have had enough of. I'll explain more about *Enough* throughout this book.

[3] Acts 6:4 (NIV).

7

overwhelming task ahead that was faced without them. So I have two key, simple proposals that need to happen for the church in the West to return to health and vitality. First, everyone needs to be a witness for Christ, through words, works and wonders. Second, everyone needs to give him or herself to corporate prayer. When both of these things become a culture, a lifestyle such that they become a "contagion" as they did in late-18th century Britain,[4] then I believe we will see a wave of church planting as a result of the numbers of people coming to Christ.

Unfortunately I also observe that these two simple but vital things are probably the weakest aspects of the western Church.

I do not consider myself to be an expert on prayer. I would not even say I am very good at prayer. I have an appetite for it, and I give myself to it as best as I can but I often lose concentration; I feel my words do not do justice to the task. I am tired easily in it. Yet I want to be on a journey with others so that together we can do things we could never otherwise do.

_____

[4] S Pearce Carey, M.A., *William Carey, D.D. Fellow of Linnean Society* (London: Hodder and Stoughton, 1923). p. 14.

I want to reach for things we had not considered possible and I have found that when I pray with others I can do better, reach higher, concentrate for longer, find words and "amen" others' prayers in a way that would simply not be possible if I were on my own.

I want corporate prayer to be accessible to all, to make it as easy as possible for people to pray. If it takes me, a fellow struggler, to be real and say, "Come on, folks, we can do this together, we really can, let's help each other" then maybe just maybe movement can occur.

There are several challenges, to any follower of Christ, to getting meaningfully engaged in the corporate prayer life of the local church, one of them being: "What difference has this made?" That's understandable, I get that. If I cook a meal, wash a car, build some furniture, paint a picture or a fence, I can almost immediately look at what I have been engaged in doing and see progress, accomplishment, achievement; fruitfulness even. Prayer is different.

Prayer often deals with unseen things and it requires eyes of faith to see what is going on. I think of a steam engine. Putting wood and coal on the fire does not immediately produce the steam that moves the engine forward. But sure enough, given repeated investment in the effort of putting more and more fuel on the fire, eventually a head of steam is built up that can move a massive hunk of steel and iron forward in a way almost unimaginable at the time of stoking the fire. Prayer does the same thing. There is a process in play before the outcome is seen; the point being that our simple words are not empty of power, they have an effect. They stir heaven into action.

To help us grasp and more fully understand these unseen realities, I have made deliberate use of imagery in each chapter. Prayer is a difficult concept to convey with words alone and so pictures and images can help. I recall being greatly impacted by an image Charles Spurgeon used of our attempts to fully understand and articulate the love of Christ for us. Spurgeon, when preaching on 30 January 1859, said:

> *None of us have ever fully comprehended the love of Christ which passeth knowledge. Philosophers have probed the earth to its very center, threaded the spheres, measured the skies, weighed the hills—nay, weighed the world itself; but this is one of those vast, boundless things, which to measure doth surpass all but the Infinite itself.*

As the swallow but skimmeth the water, and diveth not into its depths, so all the descriptions of the preacher but skim the surface, while depths immeasurable must lie far beneath our observation.[5]

I found his image of the swallow skimming the water so helpful in visualising the scale of our smallness of knowledge. So with prayer I am trying to help us see images that illustrate more than what might otherwise be conveyed through words. The soil of the heart and emotions need to be stirred for the seed of prayer to take root securely and be well watered.

My hope from this little book, is to encourage and stir further hunger for prayer as widely as possible in the Church. As Spurgeon, once again, encouraged his listeners to respond with a similar urgency:

Say to your minister, 'Sir, we must have more prayer.' Urge the people to more prayer. Have a prayer meeting, even if you have it all to yourself; and if you are asked how many were present, you can say, 'Four'. 'Four, how

---

[5] C. H. Spurgeon, 'The Shameful Sufferer', 30 January 1859 www.spurgeon.org/resource-library/sermons/the-shameful-sufferer#flipbook/

so?' 'Why, there was myself, and God the Father, and God the Son, and God the Holy Ghost; and we have had a rich and real communion together'. We must have an outpouring of real devotion, or else what is to become of many of our churches?[6]

So I hope that by the time you reach the end of this short book, you would be willing to be a part of this revolution, knowing that the fruit of your prayers and efforts might not be seen in your lifetime but knowing that this investment will produce lasting and significant change.

---

[6] C. H. Spurgeon, 'Paul's First Prayer', 25 March 1855 www.spurgeon.org/resource-library/sermons/pauls-first-prayer#flipbook/

2

DITCHES

He said, "Thus says the LORD, 'Make this valley full of trenches.' For thus says the LORD, 'You shall not see wind nor shall you see rain; yet that valley shall be filled with water, so that you shall drink, both you and your cattle and your beasts. This is but a slight thing in the sight of the LORD'"

2 KINGS 3:16-18 (NASB)

In this Old Testament story God's people are divided as a nation and compromised in their identity as Yahweh's people. This decline in their fortunes came to a crisis point as they faced a significant enemy in the King of Moab. Their very existence was once again under threat. Out of these circumstances an alliance of the kings of Judah, Israel and

Edom came into being. Sometimes it takes a serious threat to all to bring about the laying down of personal ambition, preoccupation and agenda, where God's people come together in unity in seeking God. Church history seems to suggest that a move of God occurs when the spiritual ground is almost desert-like. In such conditions, His people begin to feel parched and dry and a receptivity and responsiveness to God's Spirit returns.

Yet even with an alliance between Israel, Judah and Edom, the odds were overwhelming. The drift and decline had been so steep that they were not capable of overcoming the evil dominating the land they were in on their own. Moab was far too strong for all the resources they had at their disposal.

In this context, they ask for prophetic insight. By seeking out Elisha the prophet, they asked God what they should do. Their fundamental questions were, "Can God do something about this?", "What would God have us do?" and "Can God help us overcoming these overwhelming odds?" They realized they were outnumbered, outflanked and out of options, unless God did something about the situation.

Is this not how we feel when we look around the world as it is now? For the Church (especially in the western world) it would seem that whatever forces we might gather together, whenever we look at the news, the situation appears utterly heart-breaking. We need something that none of us have the resources for.

In this context they go to seek God through the prophet Elisha. He finally agrees, but in a surprising way, by saying "now bring me a minstrel" (musician). Why does he begin by doing this? The previous verses show that Elisha was not impressed with the leadership being given to God's people at this time. He has respect for the king of Judah but he has no regard at all for his own king, Jehoram the king of Israel, who was not leading the people in the ways of God. Elisha is only a small step from dismissing them completely but he demonstrates how to listen to God and not your own emotions.

Perhaps his call for a musician was so that he could make worship his focus. Elisha made God, not the problems, the centre of his attention. Whilst they are together Elisha puts aside the anger he was feeling, he chooses not to discuss the depleted resources and seemingly insurmountable challenges facing them and he refrains from berating them for the political nonsense they had been responsible for. He focuses on God and as the musician plays, "the hand of the Lord came upon him".

The world we live in can easily cause us to lose our focus on God. It is so vital that as we gather to pray and seek God that we come with worshipping hearts. Worship is vital in the context of prayer. We must not separate worship from prayer. Often in meetings that we call "prayer meetings" we will find much greater unction (which is a great old word for zeal and passion) in our prayers together, when we have said, as Elisha did, "bring us a minstrel".

I can you hear thinking "I thought this book was about prayer" but if in prayer we want to hear the voice of God for the urgent matters of our day, it is so important that our focus is not on those urgent matters but on God – that we come acknowledging His lordship, His sovereignty and His majesty. Having a prayer meeting well served by capable musicians is in my view vital to all else that happens. I wonder what Elisha would have done if the "minstrel" had not been there? As we together figuratively cry out "bring us a minstrel" something changes in our perspective and faith rises. Before lifting up our voices together in prayer, we lift them up together in praise. It is a great perspective changer vital to fervent, believing, collective prayer.

An army in a desert without water is an army in trouble. The food (cows, sheep and goats) would die of thirst and the soldiers would be weak and vulnerable. So the problem these three armies have, before they even face Moab in battle, is that they have no water. Elisha says "Thus says the LORD, 'Make this valley full of trenches.'"[7] Some versions say "I will make this dry streambed full of pools"[8]. The link between these slightly nuanced versions heightens the awareness of partnership. They were to prepare for God to move by digging trenches in a flatbed valley so that when God brought water all was in place for his activity to be effective. Elisha was saying "you have to do something in preparation for when God

---

[7] 2 Kings 3:16 (NASB).
[8] 2 Kings 3:16 (ESV).

17

moves". This is exactly what corporate prayer is like. It is preparing for a move of God.

Let the image shape our thinking regarding collective prayer. Prayer, like digging a ditch, requires significant effort. It is hard work. It is about turning up at the prayer meeting after a hard day at work. It is walking out the house at some unearthly hour in the morning when it is cold, dark and you can hardly remember your name let alone focus on eloquent prayers. It is giving the half night of prayer, it is raising a sweat figuratively and saying in effect "God, as we are digging these ditches in prayer we trust you that you are going to fill them up with water!" If God said to us "dig some ditches and I will move in revival power across your nation", my guess is that though it would be hard work, we would do it because of his promise. We have the equivalent promises with regard to our effort in corporate prayer.

My friend Daniel Goodman leads City Church Cambridge and I asked him how he encourages people to make the effort for our *Enough* nights of prayer. His reply is very helpful:

These evenings are important occasions. That's why I ask the church to make a special effort to be there. I am persuaded that prayer is powerful. I particularly ask everyone to come as early as possible because I want them to overlap with the children. I love it when my two boys form meaningful and fun relationships with adult Christians – it models something wonderful to them about the value of prayer and community. But it doesn't just benefit my kids, it also blesses the whole church who can really engage with disciplining the next generation!

I know it can be costly for working people to get to Enough *early in the evening. But I plead with them to do so. People will go to great lengths to be present at an important occasion. Sometimes even a few small changes to your routine can pave the way to being where you need to be. For example, I support Arsenal FC, and to get to London from Cambridge for a midweek game means I need to leave work an hour early and get straight on a train. I'm happy to do it when it feels worthwhile. How much more with occasions that are of eternal significance, such as prayer meetings? It might mean making a few slight adjustments to the routine (leaving work early, arranging a babysitter, skipping Friday night drinks etc.) but most people can do it if they choose to.*

ı

THE EARTH-MOVING POWER OF TEAMS

Films featuring the old chain gangs bound together building railway tracks or roads showed that keeping going in the heat and hard work was much easier if collectively a rhythm and a partnership were established. You and me both being there at the prayer meeting, matters as we can both be encouraged by the 'earth we move' together. Praying together is the main approach to prayer that we see in the Bible.

I noticed something Eugene Petersen said on Twitter: "In the long history of Christian spirituality, community prayer is more important than individual prayer"[9]. The more people we can mobilise in corporate prayer, the more effective the digging of ditches will be which God will fill with his answer to the need. We may each have different capacities and experience in prayer. Some may feel like they have a simple seaside bucket and spade of experience and contribution to make – hesitant, small prayers like riding a bike with stabilisers on. Maybe, for some reading this, it feels even less than that,

---

[9] Tweet by Eugene Peterson: 6.43am, 19 July 2015.

a thimble or eggcup of earth moving capability. Others you might think have great JCB earth moving capacity. Whichever it is, all prayer makes a difference and the more the better.

Whether a child or adult, a recent follower of Christ or with years of experience, it all counts, it all helps dig the ditch, you, your prayers and your presence in corporate prayer matter! I think Paul understood this when he said in 2 Corinthians 1:11 "You also must help us by prayer, so that many will give thanks on our behalf for the blessing granted us through the *prayers of many*" (italics mine). The more people praying, the more ditches dug, the more effective preparation and partnership ahead of when God moves.

Digging the ditches does not change things, only God changes things. But just as the digging of ditches in this account prepared a way for God to do what He wanted to do, so in some sovereign way, as we pray, it prepares the way for God to do what He desires to do. Whenever we pray collectively it is like we get a shovel and move earth so that there is something created in the landscape for a move of God to rest in; a ditch for water, a place for answers to prayer to land.

We see the same principle at work in Isaiah 54:2-3:

> *Enlarge the place of your tent, and let the curtains of your habitations be stretched out; do not hold back; lengthen your cords and strengthen your stakes. For you will spread abroad to the right and to the left, and your offspring will possess the nations and will people the desolate cities*

Notice what they are to do: they are to enlarge, stretch, lengthen and strengthen the tent. Why? Because God will expand and fill this enlarged tent so that the nations will know He is Lord. God called them to work in faith before God filled the space created. Prayer is about doing something ahead of what God has said he is going to do. That's how prayer works. We pray for things we have as yet not seen.

When we pray something goes on in the heavenly realms. It is every bit as real as the visible things here on Earth, but it is unseen at first, then becomes known as things change "on earth as it is in heaven". Back to the story of Elisha and the three kings – verse 17 expresses it well:

> *For thus says the LORD, 'You shall not see wind nor shall you see rain; yet that valley shall be filled with water, so*

*that you shall drink, both you and your cattle and your
beasts.'*

God promises that He is going to do something supernatural
that cannot be explained through the natural or human realms
of activity. Naturally we can say a combination of wind and
rain would ordinarily fill up ditches. Anybody could point to
a ditch filled with water in a rain storm and say "Of course it
is filled up. It has been windy and raining." God says here he
is going to fill the ditches without wind or rain. He says "I'm
going to do it so you don't know how it happened other than
by concluding 'this must be God' – that is what I am
promising." How God answers prayer cannot be explained
naturally. It cannot be explained because it is miraculous and
miracles alone belong to the Lord.

In approaching prayer, we must not be limited in our
thinking to only the way our culture thinks; rational, logical
and empirical. Ephesians 3:20 says "Now to him who is able
to do far more abundantly beyond all that we ask or think
according to the power that works within us."

God is able to go beyond the words we say or the time and effort we put in. It is not that we produce something in a formulaic way, rather we contribute obedient asking and God produces supernatural outcome. We know that the more we pray the more God will do and the more of us that pray the more effective the praying, but these are not formulaic dynamics they are relational dynamics, us and God in partnership together in his purposes across the earth.

At one of our *Enough* prayer meetings, I prayed this prayer as we live streamed across all the hubs praying: (You may wish to add your "amen" to this prayer as you read it....)

Lord we take this evening very seriously. With all the different ways we are learning how to pray and we're doing lots of fun and experimental things with prayer and we believe it all touches Your heart. Yet underlying this Lord we know this is a serious business.

We are praying for lost people. We are praying for people who we don't know if they have even got another day. We can dig ditches by our prayers but only You can fill them with water, only You – You are the sovereign Lord – only You can say 'Let there be' and there was! And we believe, we are persuaded that Your word tells us that it's Your kindness that leads us to repentance – that You are kind and loving and patient not wanting any to perish, You don't want any to perish.

We appeal to Your character and we appeal to Your nature revealed supremely to us in the person of Jesus Christ, who shows us what You are like – all the fullness of God in human flesh. Jesus, You had compassion on everyone, You were the friend of sinners. You touched the blind, healed the lame, You brought forgiveness to those whose lives were full of unrighteousness. You are the same then, today and forever. The Bible tells us so we ask You Jesus – You said You would send another just like You when You ascended to Your Father. And You sent Your Holy Spirit and He does the same thing You did, the same things in our Earth that You would do if You were here physically. So we ask that You, Holy Spirit, move across our nation, our town, move across the godless generation and thousands of people who don't know left from right who are unable to name the name of Jesus as Saviour, because they have never heard the gospel. We need You to empower us as Your people. We need You to do something that we cannot do.

We are willing, but we ask You to let the water from Heaven come that softens hearts – of neighbours, families, colleague, politicians or all that we meet, soften hearts so that gospel seed falls on good soil, so it shoots and spouts, 30, 60, 100 fold. We are asking You for a move, we're asking You to move, O God! Turn, O God! Have mercy, O God! Come upon our nation with power. As we have read and heard about – do it in our day.

We have nothing else to give You but our heartfelt cries and we raise our "amen" to You. We say Lord, look from Heaven on our weak, humble attempt. Amen.[10]

---

[10] www.vimeo.com/242567448

3
COMBAT

PRAYING TOGETHER IS LIKE
ARMED COMBAT

*Put on the whole armour of God, that you may be able
to stand against the schemes of the devil. For we do not
wrestle against flesh and blood, but against the rulers,
against the authorities, against the cosmic powers over
this present darkness, against the spiritual forces of evil in
the heavenly places. Therefore take up the whole armour
of God, that you may be able to withstand in the evil day,
and having done all, to stand firm.*

EPHESIANS 6:11-13 (ESV)

The Old Testament often highlights quite unusual individuals
who single handed gained victory; Moses against Pharaoh,
Samson against the Philistines and of course David against
Goliath. Once we arrive at the New Testament the anointed

individual seems to give way in emphasis to the anointed body of Christ; the church.

In the West our individualistic culture often causes us to view things in the singular by default and see things only as they apply to us as individuals. It's vital to recognise that we together, the church, form the body of Christ. We together are a royal priesthood, a holy nation. It is our oneness that is the emphasis in the New Testament. Our combat is effective through our togetherness. The church should not look for individual superheroes but we should look for a united and equipped 'body' – the church.

Here there is a collective combat scene in mind. Why? Military history tells us that battles fought by armies outnumbered and outgunned mostly end in defeat or retreat. Paul informs us our foe is not simply flesh and blood, which we could take on, on equal terms. Instead we fight huge forces of evil far too big for us to overcome on our own. An individual Christian filled with the Holy Spirit can pray and see demonic oppression be lifted from another individual. Jesus both did this himself and trained his disciples to do it, saying all who followed him would be equipped to engage successfully in such things.

What Ephesians 6 refers to are principalities and powers, huge demonic powers over areas, nations, cultures. One person is not sufficient on their own to engage with such things. It would be folly. That is why we "wrestle". These verses have often been applied to individual Christians. Live life alert and prepared for our own individual battles with the world, the flesh and the devil. However, we must not overlook the inherently corporate nature of these verses. Notice the "we"? "For *we* do not wrestle…" It is not weakness to rightly discern our enemy and know when single handed combat is not how God intends us to fight certain battles.

In Acts 12 we find Peter asleep and in prison. This was not peacetime season and as in times of war the whole nation helps out. So as Peter faced a moment of exceptional difficulty, he needed more than his own effort in a personal prayer time. Great effort was required on his behalf. Peter needed reinforcements.

King Herod Agrippa was being "violent"[11] against the church and the church was becoming violent with a different kind of force. A force so great it brought about a dispatch of angelic visitation and a miracle prison break for Peter. Prayer is not an attempt at consolation when facing defeat, it is a mighty weapon. When the church prays, the heavens roar and demons quake yet we are all too often unaware of these dynamics. But they are real and should make us treat prayer for what it is: a powerful force.

Peter was in prison, it was the church that was praying on his behalf for of his release. His release was secured not by his own prayers (he was in fact asleep while others were praying) but by the collective prayer of the church on his behalf. They, in effect, locked shields in prayer together for him and saw their combat effective for his release.

Today such extraordinary scheduling of a whole church, being invited to join in prayer together, in response to sickness, crisis or overwhelming circumstances is vital. We must never programme or plan church life to such an extent

---

[11] Acts 12:1 (ESV).

that, when we encounter enemy action in unforeseen events, there is no space to respond. No army ever won a battle without having the flexibility to fight as present circumstances dictate.

Ben Parish, who leads the eldership team at my own church in Lowestoft, gives this example:

The news came through during a January week of prayer that the church was holding that one of our members, Jimmi Clarke, was suddenly diagnosed with stomach cancer. There are times as a local church when you need to gather together in numbers to pray for breakthrough in a situation, like an army launching an assault on enemy territory and this felt like one of those times. We sent the message round that the final planned evening of prayer was going to specifically be to pray over Jimmi and seek his healing. It was incredible to see how the church family rallied around and much fervent prayer was given to see the cancer go and Jimmi's health restored. Whilst on that occasion an instant miracle didn't take place, Jimmi testifies that the combative prayers of many friends, family and Christians all around the globe saw him and his family through that time and he is now, wonderfully, in full health.

It is perhaps relatively easy to imagine that the church would respond positively when faced with dramatic and out of the ordinary situations. Yet we also need to sustain the offensive through regular times of gathered prayer.

THE TESTUDO EFFECT

Roman soldiers had become almost invincible on the battlefield through a technique named after the humble tortoise. Known as the "Testudo" (tortoise) formation soldiers would link their shields to give an appearance similar to the shell of a tortoise. Such linking through team work brought huge advantages when in battle both for protection and advance.

I recall a very powerful moment in a meeting of network leaders: we had all shared various news and prayer points from our different settings; I had spoken of a season of what felt like sustained pressure and significant challenge – this season had left me feeling quite depleted in spiritual energy, fight and quite fearful if I am honest. This group of leaders gathered round me and took authority over that which had been coming against me. Prophesies and powerful declarations of victory filled the meeting. I felt and knew a surge of spiritual power in that moment the like of which was of another level to anything I would have been able to do myself and for myself. I felt something broke in the heavenly realms. We need each other to pray for each other.... Testudo!!

If I push the Roman army analogy a little further then each local church is a regiment to bring God's rule and order in to the community whether locally, regionally, nationally or even internationally. To form our own prayer 'testudo' is a mighty advantage in our spiritual battle to see the gospel advance and men and women come to know Christ.

John Sutcliffe was a contemporary of William Carey, from Olney Baptist. Speaking of the reality of spiritual conflict and the vital nature of corporate prayer in tackling it, he said:

> ...all should remember, that there are but two parties in the world, each engaged in opposite causes; the cause of God and the cause of Satan; the cause of holiness and sin; of heaven and hell. The advancement of one and the downfall of the other, must appear exceedingly desirable to every real friend of God and man...Oh, for thousands upon thousands divided into small bands in their

*respective cities, towns, villages and neighbourhood, all
met at the same time and in pursuit of the one end,
offering up their united prayers, like so many ascending
clouds of incense before the Most High.* [12]

In my own local church as an eldership team we felt it right to
commence a Friday lunchtime prayer time for one hour
together. Not everyone can make it each time, but those that
can will gather, fast for the lunchtime and simply pray
together for God to move. Just imagine the impact we would
see if across many church leadership teams began to do similar
things. Imagine a situation where with a minimum of
organization, planning and infrastructure, Friday lunchtimes
became places where a simple one hour fasting and calling on
God for Him to move grew and grew across a nation.

To quote the song – "there's an army rising up, to break
every chain"[13] – this captures the essence of corporate prayer

---

[12] John Sutcliffe, Preface to Jonathan Edwards' 'An Humble
Attempt' in Edward Hickman (ed.) *The Works of Jonathan Edwards
Vol 1 & 2*. (Banner of Truth Trust, 1974) p432.

[13] Will Reagan and United Pursuit, 'Break Every Chain'. From
the album *In the Night Season*, 2009.

seen as combat perfectly. The shields in such formation are both defensive. They were often soaked in water so as to extinguish fiery arrows that may have been fired at them. Ephesians talks of extinguishing the enemy's "fiery darts". The shields enabled strategic advance that would not be possible by one person on their own.

We can find that when others join in praying with us, suddenly something else kicks in. As we pray collectively, helping each other, issuing an "amen" to each other's requests, then once more an energy that isn't from our own resources comes into play. This is Holy Spirit weaponry coming into play: reinforcements arriving to a beleaguered, under-siege, outpost of heaven.

As a family of churches in *Relational Mission* a few years ago we felt it right to commence half nights of prayer across the whole family of churches. We started gathering three times a year, in geographic hubs, at the same time, on the same date, in different locations, to pray about the same things. This initiative called *Enough* has been growing and at the time I write we are presently seeing this expand to involve others beyond our own group of churches. This initiative was the response to a prompting of God to gather in large numbers and in my own humble opinion, the larger the better.

The devil tries to cover up the battle that is going on. If he can persuade us it is peacetime when we are in fact at war, then he has scored a major tactical victory. Satan is a subversive, tactical and hidden yet present enemy. If we fight the forces of darkness we win, if we don't we will face avoidable losses. War is like that. We may feel we are outnumbered and outgunned sometimes. The devil and his forces are more powerful than we humans. However, we have all of the resources/energy of the Holy Spirit to help us pray and to answer our prayers. We do not fight with human energy rather we draw from another realm.

A little child when it meets enemies, or fierce beasts, is not apt to trust its own strength, but flies to its parents: for refuge so a saint is not self-confident in engaging spiritual enemies, but flies to Christ.[14]

---

[14] Jonathan Edwards, 'A treatise concerning religious affections in three parts', Part 3 Section IX – 'Gracious affections soften the heart, and are attended with a Christian tenderness of Spirit' in

Prayer works because in doing it we are both doing something (asking of the Lord) in obedience that has been urged of us and we are asking one who is more than capable of not only doing all we are asking, but more than we have asked or can even imagine (Ephesians 3:20). Praying together enables us to press in by faith to the throne of God even when we feel tired, weak and out of sorts. We carry one another in.

At times, it can feel a bit awkward asking for prayer, especially as a leader. Yet Paul often writes to his churches saying "please pray for me". In 2 Corinthians 7:5 Paul writes, "For even when we came into Macedonia, our bodies had no rest, but we were afflicted at every turn—fighting without and fear within."

This is why Paul often asked for prayer for himself. He knew he faced principalities and powers far bigger than he could handle on his own.

Edward Hickman (ed.), *The Works of Jonathan Edwards Vol 1*. (Banner of Truth Trust, 1974) p. 308.

> *"You also must help us by prayer, so that many will give*
> *thanks on our behalf for the blessing granted us through*
> *the prayers of many."*
>
> 2 CORINTHIANS 1:11

His awareness was that numbers of people engaging in corporate prayer regularly and continually for him was crucial to success in his apostolic mission.

Whenever an individual or team set out to take new ground whether planting a church, establishing a new kingdom ministry in the local community, standing up for kingdom values in the workplace or wider society, we need the Testudo effect. We cannot ask people to step out unless we have in place strategic corporate prayer to give them the prayer warrior support they need as they advance.

The term "brothers-in-arms" has been used of those who have fought together on the battlefield. They find that things were forged in combat, that have created a very deep commitment to each other relationally and in the cause. As such a life-long bond is often formed by those who have placed their lives in each other's hands and been on the same campaign. Any church that has planted numbers of churches or touched nations with mission endeavour or taken on a large building project will know the huge collective effort in prayer that will have been required to see these things birthed and fruitful. Such 'warlike' effort forms deep bonds in a church collectively.

Sometimes it seems like we have lost ground or lost a key piece of ground. Sometimes we pray and the situation does not change or even at times seems to get worse. Not all battles are won in the immediate. We do have to live with warlike dynamics with regard to apparent casualties and setbacks.

PRAYER IS THE HEAVY WEAPONRY

A setback, an apparent defeat or delay, must be approached in the same way an army would approach it. We feel its impact, assess the situation, regroup, rethink and then redeploy. Often the most seemingly impenetrable stronghold, that has resisted many attempts, will one day yield to those who remain relentless, courageous, unflinching, confident in the resources they have and certain of the cause they are fighting for. Never give up.

*Continue steadfastly in prayer, being watchful in it with
thanksgiving. At the same time, pray also for us, that God
may open to us a door for the word, to declare the mystery
of Christ, on account of which I am in prison.*

COLOSSIANS 4:2-3 (ESV)

The reality is that the war mostly certainly has been won. Jesus
has already established the victory. We fight now with Him to
establish the outworking of the victory gained on the cross.
That it may be "on earth as it is in heaven". There is a lot of
territory to be taken by Him, with Him, and through Him –
one heart at a time, yielding to the Saviour.

If we take seriously the Bible's imagery of spiritual battles
then we need to realise that prayer is our heavy weaponry. It
needs to be on the front line and not in the refreshment tent.
If we feel we are besieged by the surrounding culture then as
we pray we begin to realise that it is quite the reverse. We are
in fact bringing the strongholds of godlessness under siege.
How is your church outworking its prayer strategy? Is the
heavy weaponry on the front line?

Our ultimate confidence is not in our praying but in the
power and authority of Christ who has and will crush all our

enemies under His feet. Prayer engages in partnership with Christ. Christ redeemed man and raised him to rule and reign with Him. We are now seated with Christ. We share in His inheritance. Christ is our elder brother. We are in the 'family' business. It is from this position we rule and reign with Him.

As co-heirs with Him we have the privilege and right to ask of Him in prayer. Prayer is the means Christ has ordained for the release of His power and authority into any and all situations. Prayer enables a sovereign partnership in combat, but it is not one we have initiated but is rather our response to our commanding officer, the captain of the army, the Lord of hosts.

> *Thus says the LORD to you, 'Do not be afraid and do not be dismayed at this great horde, for the battle is not yours but God's.'*
>
> 2 CHRONICLES 20:15

The battle really does belong to the Lord. We are not caught in some sort of dualism where the outcome is uncertain. We are not persuading God to aid us and fight for us when He is actually quite reluctant. He is more aware of and engaged in the battle than we shall ever be. He fought on the cross and won. We are now joining in with the relentless advance of His kingdom being worked out through all nations as He is establishing His kingdom and brings all things under His feet. We ask of Christ and He steps in as our deliverer.

4

FIRE

CORPORATE PRAYER IS LIKE KINDLING A FIRE

When the day of Pentecost arrived, they were all together in one place. And suddenly there came from heaven a sound like a mighty rushing wind, and it filled the entire house where they were sitting. And divided tongues as of fire appeared to them and rested on each one of them. And they were all filled with the Holy Spirit and began to speak in other tongues as the Spirit gave them utterance.

ACTS 2:1-4

One of the most enjoyable aspects of the winter season to my mind is lighting and being warmed by a fire in the little wood-burner we have in our house. There is something fascinating and mesmerizing about a fire. It not only warms the body but often the thoughts and emotions as well. A good fire needs the right fuel, takes time to build, and takes a little planning to get going well. A good fire needs space around the structure to allow the fire to build up heat. It takes time to build momentum

I believe we have to build a culture of corporate prayer once more in the western Church. This is not an event. It is a process. It cannot be rushed. It is as though the wood has got wet and needs drying out. I sometimes think it could take the rest of my lifetime to really see the fire catch hold in the way I believe God intends. No matter, I am happy to be a fire starter in some small way.

Just as a fire in my wood-burner takes a little planning, patience and the right fuel, so does a prayer meeting. Planning, patience, fuel, spaces to let the flames and heat build. I am not talking of whipping up emotion. Rather I am suggesting that there is a way to allow the Holy Spirit to build prayer meetings into something where He is decisively active in them.

How is this done? The passages above show dynamics between God and man in the context of prayer. People position themselves in prayer and God responds with His manifest presence. We must not only maintain good teaching and practice with regard to being baptised with the Holy Spirit but also teach people how to go on being filled. The more familiarity we cultivate with the Holy Spirit and His ways, the more easily a prayer meeting will flow in the Holy Spirit. The baptism of the Holy Spirit surely must affect the gathered prayer life of the church.

Prayer meetings provide an opportunity for people to learn how to flow in the gifts and ministry of the Spirit. Unlike a Sunday morning, which can include a full programme, prayer meetings, in my experience, tend to have less structure / allow space and can and should give room for the manifest presence of God.

FIRE IS NOT TIDY

Corporate prayer is messy, untidy and difficult to airbrush. Fire is not tidy especially when the sparks are flying. Sometimes contributions are a bit off-key and occasionally embarrassing. If we have sanitized church to make it look slick all the time, we have lost not only the rawness of human interaction with God but we have lost what family is all about as church. The church is not a West End show and it's not a business showpiece with a keynote talk. It is a family and it is more akin to a Christmas dinner table gathering than a formal dinner jacket affair.

Fire is not tidy or predictable; fire burns and consumes. If you're someone who has the privilege of leading a prayer meeting then I want to encourage you to allow mistakes in prayer meetings and not be troubled by contributions that have nothing to do with what everyone else is praying about. Let it go and move on. It's easier to work with a church that has passion that needs directing than a church that has order but needs passion.

In my experience one of the best ways to see people grow in their gifting, in their passion for Christ and His purposes, in their recognition and responsiveness to the Holy Spirit and His activity is to expose them to and involve them in corporate prayer meetings. Leaders, church planters, evangelists, those empowering the poor and prophets can all be born in a prayer meeting. Prayer meetings alive with the manifest presence of God cannot help but affect those who are there, and many of those who are not, as prayer is answered. It's a win-win. People learn how to pray and to care about the things God cares about by being in prayer meetings. Fire spreads to other wood, even damp wood hisses a bit but eventually gets caught up in the fire. Churches that are perhaps finding charismatic life to be flagging, can find them re-energised by hosting prayer meetings.

My wood-burner has a metal outer case; that's what makes it safe. If the fire was on the carpet it would be dangerous. An out of control fire will burn your house down. Leadership and authority rightly create a place of safety where the fire can be lit and it can roar in great safety. Through good and God-appointed leadership the boundaries are constructed to make the fire burn well so people have light and heat but don't get burnt.

Planning a prayer meeting is so important: the content, timing, pace, leadership and flow of the meeting are crucial. We would not dream of turning up to a Sunday morning without any planning whatsoever of the content, shape and timings of the meeting. Why should we think prayer meetings require any less focus or diligence? Leading a prayer meeting requires high calibre spiritual leadership from those with that responsibility. The skill in leading a meeting is almost to make it feel like it is not being led, with seamless transitions between content and easy flow to the meeting.

One church that has re-invested in corporate prayer has been Hope Church in Ipswich. I'll let Tom Scrivens, the lead elder of Hope Church explain:

Over the past few years Hope Church has seen rather significant growth. Having multiplied to two services, we prayed as leaders and sought God for our longer term direction and felt prompted to seek Him for larger premises. With next to nothing in the bank we had no choice but to pray and so we embarked on a journey in corporate prayer.

In January 2016 we began 'Prayer & Vision' nights on the first Wednesday of each month, breaking with this pattern only to accommodate the Enough *half nights of prayer. We called off midweek groups to ensure maximum attendance – any groups discovered to be meeting on such weeks would risk incurring the wrath of the elders!*

From occasional prayer nights where a couple of dozen would attend, we now see upwards of 100 attend our Prayer & Vision nights and whilst we'd love to see more coming along, we have seen the church's appetite for praying together grow hugely. Along the way we've seen God do some incredible things in answer to prayer!

A key for us has been to cast vision for these evenings in our preaching. Church leaders need to be realistic about 'notices' – usually this is switch-off time for the congregation as the dates and event details are available elsewhere. Strategic preach planning has been crucial and we almost always preach on prayer on the Sunday beforehand, which will include an appeal to join us at the Prayer & Vision night.

We've been intentional in other ways and this has contributed to the momentum of these evenings. We've held our meetings in the main auditorium (capacity 200) and with a full band to lead us in praise before we pray. This sends the message to the church that we're expecting many to be present, whereas to meet in a side room and a much reduced band would send a different message.

Over the course of these two and a half years we've covered a lot of what we do in fervent prayer and we're seeing that it works! We've recently moved to a new way of doing group and it has meant that our pattern of Prayer & Vision nights has changed, but we're more convinced than ever that these are the 'events' that truly drive our church forward in God's purposes – they are absolutely vital!"

FUELLING PRAYER

We can all too easily think that fire and structure are in conflict but that's just not the case – planning to pray should fuel the fire not put it out! I'm going to keep pushing the fire analogy (I might break it but you'll get the point): a fire starts well when it has dry and not damp wood. A prayer meeting starts well when hearts are open and ready for God to move with the expectation that God is there. A fire grows when there is a good structure of kindling wood around a firelighter. A prayer meeting grows well a solid agenda for prayer is set out. Timing is important, let it build, blow on it, open the vents to let the small fire spread and flow. Sometimes it just takes time to get it going. A fire can even go out a few times and need quite a bit of attention in the early stages. This dynamic is not just about each prayer meeting but building a culture of prayer in a church of movement. It takes patience, time, method and focus but prayer, like fire, once lit, spreads.

We often can pray ourselves into prayer. I can recall many early-morning prayer meetings when I have left the house in winter half asleep and began the prayer meeting still half asleep. But as the fire grows, I often found there is a moment when someone prays something and something comes alight in my spirit and often it is obvious everyone else has felt the same thing. I'm not alone in having that experience, as Daniel Goodman from City Church Cambridge says:

I've never regretted praying. That isn't to say that I don't sometimes find it hard to pray, or that I'm not tempted to stay home from time to time but, when I've prayed I'm always glad I did. Some of the best prayer meetings I've been part of have been ones where it feels like everyone is pulling in the same direction. Maybe a better way of saying that is that everyone is being drawn in the same direction. I think this happens when there is great unity of heart. You may not know everyone, or even all speak the same languages but you know that you're all on the same journey and the prayers just seem to flow.

There are so many creative ways to pray! I think some of my favourite times together have been when we've been involved in prayer in a different way than I'm used to! Prayer times for us have involved postcards, pictures, paper aeroplanes, pick n' mix and puzzles, to name but a few examples!

51

It's also encouraging when you see the impact of your prayers in an immediate way. On one occasion, someone urgently felt that we should pray for a particular family in Sweden. We found out later that that entire family had been in a serious car crash five minutes after we had prayed but that everyone in the family (pregnant mother included!) were safe. That's the power of prayer in real time!

We can learn how to observe and flow with a theme that develops. A subject is introduced, a song is sung, a spiritual gift (tongues, prophecy) is exercised: the Holy Spirit is prompting something. One prays, others sense in their hearts an "amen", a burden, an emotion around what is being prayed for. Another prays in the flow of this theme, the room gets louder as the "amen"s get added with more sense of force. Prayers leap, one after another, like fire as it catches on the small kindling that sparked it. Someone prays out loud for the first time, this energizes the room yet further and the intensity increases. Another song picks up the theme, a wave of praying all out loud altogether in native tongues to those present and mixes with the gift of tongues as people overflow beyond what they can pray for with their mind.

Like Paul they begin to pray with their spirit, both with understanding and beyond understanding. It all flows together. Silence descends, we wait, pause, there is expectation and reflection. Another subject is mentioned by the prayer meeting leader, a quicker leaping of the flames of prayer springs up. Again and again the cycle is repeated: thanksgiving, worship, supplication and intercession, asking, asking and asking. Where did the time go? Now that is a prayer meeting!

I have been in some wonderful prayer meetings where the presence of God was very striking; they remain etched on my memory. One such meeting was in Kenya. I have rarely met such intensity of intercession. This was not a hyped atmosphere. It began as our fire analogy illustrates, in a steady gentle way. At one point though the room erupted in what seems like hours long but was probably about 15 minutes of fervent calling on God all together.

In that context amongst all the noise God spoke very deeply and personally to me about something He wanted me to do with Him. I always find it amazing that God is able to speak in a still small voice even in the midst of lots of noise! The church in the Global South and East has much to teach the church in the West about prayer. It is not about copying style, it is about replicating values. Those who believe in prayer, pray! The West, generally, is immersed in dependence on the logical, the empirical, the cognitive. Too many of us in the West find it hard to connect with the spiritual side of things. Perhaps we need some cultural strongholds in our thinking to be changed.

5

ORCHESTRA

CORPORATE PRAYER IS LIKE
AN ORCHESTRA PLAYING

Blow the trumpet in Zion;
consecrate a fast;
call a solemn assembly;
gather the people.
Consecrate the congregation;
assemble the elders;
gather the children,
even nursing infants.
Let the bridegroom leave his room,
and the bride her chamber.

JOEL 2:15-16

In my study amongst the books, papers, laptop and so on I have a small tuning fork. It's the note A, I believe. I have it there to remind me that as I do my best to serve the church I am required by the Lord to make sure that whatever I teach, build, practice, say, display and encourage is all in alignment with both the scriptures and the work of the Holy Spirit. As anyone who has heard a live band can testify: keeping things in tune is vital to a beautiful melody.

I love music, nearly all kinds, especially jazz. It is a genre of music that in my view most displays the fusion between unbending principles and individual creativity. For jazz to work the musicians must be in the same key as each other but jazz gives space for each musician to play off of each other, each one supporting the person who is taking the lead at that time. Not everyone improvises all at once but rather different musicians take the lead at different parts of the piece.

In a symphony, the conductor brings in various instruments at various times. Sometimes a solo piece draws our attention. In Joel where we read "blow the trumpet", there was a distinctive rallying call – if you like, a piece in the symphony inviting the engagement of others rather than applause for the soloist. Sometimes a conductor will seem like he is bringing in every instrument, unleashing a crescendo of great power and emotion, harmonies, rhythms, and melodic tunes. This is like

Acts 4 when they raised their voices all together crying out to God. Somehow their prayers were so aligned that the totality of the content and theme could be summarized in one thread "Sovereign Lord, who made the heaven…".[15]

Music, played by multiple musicians, is very much like how a good prayer meeting can and should flow – emotion, content, same key, same pace, unity and harmony, agreement of content and style. It is interesting that Jonathan Edwards referred to these widespread prayer meetings as a "concert of prayer".[16] The musical comparison was not lost on him. Continuing this metaphor further, what are some of the comparisons and applications with music and corporate prayer?

PRAYING IN TUNE

Prayer, effective prayer, requires us to be in tune with each other. No discord or disunity. Unity is not firstly about having

---

[15] Acts 4:24 (ESV).
[16] Jonathan Edwards, *A Call to United Extraordinary Prayer: An Humble attempt…* (James Nisbett, 1831), p. 61.

people geographically in the same place doing the same thing, though at times this may be an expression of the deeper meaning of unity. Neither is unity about papering over issues that need addressing.

Unity is instead nurtured through heart agreement, affection, love and honour for the body of Christ. Psalm 133 indicates that such unity is conducive to God initiating blessing. Jesus' main prayer for His church is found in John 17 where Jesus prays repeatedly in several verses "that they may be one". Jesus deliberately says this part of His prayer is not only for His small band of current disciples but "for those who will believe in me through their word". He is praying for a future aspect of His church. Such an important theme to Him must not pass us by quickly. What matters to Him should matter to us also.

We also find in Ephesians 4 the encouragement to "maintain" unity in the church. Paul then gives a broad, sweeping overview of what Christ is doing in his universal church. This is worked out in each local church but Paul's point is clear: unity in the church matters.

One of the best ways to build unity is to pray together. Praying has a way of joining hearts that might not otherwise be joined. There will be numbers of different doctrines and practices within local churches so working out unity is not always easy. It's important for leaders to be clear about the authentic gospel, and "unite" all believers in prayer and mission from a common understanding of the gospel. Then they can pray with a united desire to see the gospel spreading locally nationally and internationally.

Augustine said "In essentials, unity; in nonessentials, liberty; in all things, love."[17]

John Wesley, no stranger to disagreement with gospel partners said, "Though we cannot think alike, may we not love alike? May we not be of one heart, though we are not of one opinion? Without all doubt, we may. Herein all the children of God may unite, notwithstanding these smaller differences."[18]

---

[17] Quote widely attributed to Augustine.

[18] John Wesley, Sermon 39 – 'Catholic Spirit' in Thomas Jackson (ed.), *Complete Works* (Zondervan Publishing House, 1872), page unknown.

When hearts begin to be softened and turned toward each other; when leaders begin to care for, pray for and desire to see blessing come upon other leaders in other churches, you know then that the ground is being prepared for a more significant moving of the Holy Spirit. A common feature of genuine revival is that unity across a wide range of churches is visible and heartfelt. A softening of hearts leads to listening and appreciating one another which leads to praying together and as we pray God begins to move. I would observe that the further a society moves away from God's good order and changes its moral compass the more evident the lostness and hopelessness. Eventually this greater need begins to govern the thinking of the church more than our minor (though important) intra-church differences. The agenda becomes "God we need you to have mercy on our nation". The issues that once seemed crucial to unity become secondary compared to the desperate condition of souls travelling in droves into a Christ-less eternity.

One of the things I have observed in the West in recent years has been the emergence of prayer movements that cross different streams, networks and denominations. In our own

Enough initiative we have begun to see others who are not part of our family of churches expressing interest in joining in. I love this and celebrate the fact that God does seem to be helping the church recover the joy and power of large-scale corporate prayer. I would love to see the 2000 we began our *Enough* initiative with become 20,000 praying people across different time zones, places, churches and languages, yet all praying as Jonathan Edwards said: "for the awakening of the church in our town and beyond. And the spread of the kingdom of God worldwide."[19] What a prayer agenda. What a concert!

Yet unity is not only something expressed between churches but must first of all be expressed within a local church. Effectiveness in corporate prayer in a local church is closely linked with unity within that church. We are fighting the same enemy and if the devil, through the activities of his demons, can divide the body of Christ he knows he will hinder prayer.

---

[19] Ben Patterson paraphrases Edwards, 'Adventures in Fasting', *Christianity Today*, 2 March 1998
www.christianitytoday.com/ct/1998/march2/8t3048.html

I believe he fears corporate prayer more than almost anything else and this is why the devil attacks unity so much. He looks to create divisions in any corporate dynamic, whether between husband and wife or within leadership teams or amongst the wider church. Fractured relationships hinder the effectiveness of corporate prayer.

In a local church that normalises unresolved issues and brushes things under the carpet, a trend will develop which creates a culture or stronghold within the church. It will be very hard for corporate prayer to be effective, because there is only surface unity.

Ephesians 4:26 says "Do not let the sun go down on your anger." This is the principle we must operate out of. Pay attention to matters that affect local church unity. Don't let, in this case, "anger" remain in place unresolved and fermenting.

The Bible is clear that there are two courses of action. Firstly, find grace to process it between you and God.

A person's wisdom yields patience; it is to one's glory to overlook an offense.

PROVERBS 19:11

Fools show their annoyance at once, but the prudent overlook an insult.

PROVERBS 12:16

Secondly, if it becomes clear there is an issue internally that just won't go away, then follow the biblical pattern and talk to the person concerned, as in Matthew 18:15 (ESVUK): "If your brother sins against you, go and tell him his fault, between you and him alone. If he listens to you, you have gained your brother."

The reason these issues matter, is that the Holy Spirit can move unhindered where hearts are right with God and right with each other. Prayer meetings can be places where issues get sorted out. Often as we pray together, forgiveness and unity can descend. I was in a prayer meeting recently where two leaders who had been holding different opinions on a strategic matter for some years suddenly felt the Holy Spirit move upon them and melt their hearts for each other's blessing. They prayed for each other and released each other into the callings they both felt right to do. As a result of the Holy Spirit moving in a prayer meeting, suddenly many meetings to try and sort this out were bypassed. The tuning fork in God's hand had brought harmony from discord. Attitude matters as if it is wrong it is like music out of tune.

> *First of all, then, I urge that supplications, prayers, intercessions, and thanksgivings be made for all people, for kings and all who are in high positions, that we may lead a peaceful and quiet life, godly and dignified in every way. This is good, and it is pleasing in the sight of God our Saviour...*
>
> 1 TIMOTHY 2:1-3

> *Since prayer is at the bottom of all this, what I want mostly is for men to pray—not shaking angry fists at enemies but raising holy hands to God. And I want women to get in there with the men in humility before God, not primping before a mirror or chasing the latest fashions but doing something beautiful for God and becoming beautiful doing it.*
>
> 1 TIMOTHY 2:8 (MSG)

When Paul is writing about key values and activities local churches should engage in he says corporate prayer is a key element but more than that, prayer in the right attitude. The condition of our hearts does affect the outcome of our prayers. He also references that the things we pray for from "all people", right through to "Kings and all those in high positions" are how we should engage with politics and current affairs. Rather than developing cynical, sarcastic and overly critical hearts to all that is going on in the world around us, we should instead be so convinced that the best way to change things is to pray, that we avoid wasting time, effort and words on saying how bad things are and instead pour out intercession to God confident that he can and will change things. Engage with politics through prayer not cynical satire.

DEVOTION AND DISCIPLINE

Musicians love music; whilst they might be fond of a particular favourite instrument, it is a means to an end. It is the love of music that warrants the instrument. In the same way, we do not love corporate prayer, we love the Lord, and our prayers are a way to express our love for Him and draw

65

nearer to Him. This makes the effort required to pray more about the relationship than the act itself. Luciano Pavarotti said "People think I'm disciplined. It is not discipline. It is devotion. There is a great difference."[20] Our devotion is to the Lord, not to corporate prayer.

Each prayer meeting should and will feel different. It is like an engagement of musicians (the church) and the conductor (the Holy Spirit). We should prepare well. An orchestra does not play well, however good the conductor is, if there is not order and preparation for the concert. I believe prayer meetings need the most rigorous and detailed planning of all church meetings, yet we must also feel free to abandon our plans and submit to the Holy Spirit's leading.

The point of planning is not to follow the plan rigidly but to create a context where it is easy for God to move by His Spirit as we pray. Our plans yield to His, allowing space for something to develop and flow. We need discernment as to what God is doing in a meeting in order for this to happen.

---

[20] Luciano Pavarotti, *Pavarotti, My Own Story* (Doubleday, 1981), page unknown.

As musicians play, it evokes emotions from the conductor, the audience and other musicians. Everyone involved feels emotionally affected by someone else's feelings being conveyed through their music. Prayers are no different. I can recall many times I have been moved very deeply listening to someone else pray in a prayer meeting. It is like they touch something in my heart that resonates with their prayer. Not only so but we are told that our conductor the Holy Spirit also feels affected in the context of our prayer meetings. The Amplified Bible translation of Romans 8:26 expresses this very fully:

> *In the same way the Spirit [comes to us and] helps us in our weakness. We do not know what prayer to offer or how to offer it as we should, but the Spirit Himself [knows our need and at the right time] intercedes on our behalf with sighs and groaning's too deep for words.*

Both He and we all feel the emotion.

I remember well, some years ago, when our local church was in its infancy, an evening when the youth group (at that time I was a part it) met at someone's small terraced house. So many people gathered that they were sitting in both front and back rooms and up the stairs to the landing. We began a time of prayer and worship, seeking God for his presence and purposes to unfold in the coming days. At one point a worship song came to an end and spontaneously in one room a few people began to sing in the Spirit using the gift of tongues. Their prayers to God in an unknown language began to spread as others in that room began to join in. Soon a wave of sound flowed like a pair of stereo speakers between the two rooms then up and down the stairs as wave upon wave of unrehearsed and, at that time, very unusual prayers in tongues swept through the house. It felt just like a conductor waving his baton over a choir. The beauty, harmony, unity, power and emotion were something I have never forgotten. This collective impact was then followed by numbers of people praying in English for God to move. In this moment, I believe they were bringing a collective sense of what the Holy Spirit had been moving us to pray for. It was like a corporate interpretation – praise God!

I think we often fail to recognize what happens after "collective singing in the Spirit" as it is often called. I believe often God brings, as in Acts 4, a summary of what has been prayed collectively. These moments when God breaks in unexpectedly must be stewarded well. Such times cannot be planned for and our plans must yield when things like this happen. It is like a jazz virtuoso piece from heaven, which suddenly takes centre stage.

Unity is the orchestra getting in tune with each other. Careful planning and preparation is the necessary practice for the musicians. Openness to the leading of the Spirit allows the great conductor to lead us. When it all comes together in the context of a church at prayer it is a beautiful sound and one I believe is pleasing to our Lord.

6
FAMILY
CORPORATE PRAYER WORKS WITH FAMILY DYNAMICS

For this reason I kneel before the Father, from whom every family in heaven and on earth derives its name. I pray that out of his glorious riches he may strengthen you with power through his Spirit in your inner being, so that Christ may dwell in your hearts through faith.

EPHESIANS 3:14-17A

When we pray together we gather as to a Father round a warm fire, listening, talking and being together. Isaiah 1:18 says "'Come now, let us reason together,' says the LORD". As we pray together God reveals His heart to His children. He counsels us on family matters not as servants who do not know his master's business rather as we are: co-heirs with Christ. We are those who have a claim to the divine promises of scripture and share in His nature. We have, through Christ, the family likeness. We pray from who we are as well as from what we are not. We may pray out of longing to be someone or something but we should also pray because in Christ we are now someone; we are now a child of the King.

This is all because salvation is relational. Through receiving Christ, God has become our Father. Our relationships with His people are family relationships. We are God's children not his employees. Ephesians 3:15 says "from whom every family in heaven and on earth is named". This family dynamic should flavour all aspects of our corporate prayer life as this chapter seeks to explore.

There are many verses in the New Testament instructing us as to how we should be with "one another"; love, encourage, admonish, care for, etc. It should not take a programmed corporate prayer meeting to develop a lifestyle of prayer for and with one another. The spontaneous buzz of pre or post meeting conversations, refreshments mingled with one and twos praying together is a culture to be prized. The way we pray together is important. When we receive prayer we need an open receptive stance inwardly receiving from the Lord. When we pray for others we are serving them, not imposing an agenda on them or trying to score 'prayer answered' points. Let us strive for a relational culture where a church family does life together and in the midst of that we find it as natural to pray for each other as we would to share a cup of coffee. We don't want to trivialise prayer but to normalise it.

Even as I am writing this a few messages have come through concerning immediate things that were of concern. I stopped typing, updated my wife and together we for a few minutes brought these situations to the Lord. It is not about the length of time we pray, but making it an instinctive habit in everything to pray. Knowing we are coming to the one who does more than all we ask of imagine is a great boost to any praying soul.

Specific examples are given in scripture of this kind of family dynamic regarding the ups and downs of life, as well as when we are facing specific issues of sickness and affected by sin.

> *Is anyone among you sick? Let him call for the elders of the church, and let them pray over him, anointing him with oil in the name of the Lord*
>
> JAMES 5:14

72

Therefore, confess your sins to one another and pray for one another, that you may be healed. The prayer of a righteous person has great power as it is working.

JAMES 5:16

Rejoice with those who rejoice, weep with those who weep.

ROMANS 12:15

I can recall numbers of occasions through the years when a troubled heart has led me to discuss the matter with trusted brothers in the church. Somehow talking things through and then praying together is a very powerful way of getting breakthrough. Confessing and being transparent and accountable to another is freeing. These issues are not always obvious sin, but can just as likely be concern, temptation, worry or struggling to see a way through complex issues. I have both sought and given help in this way over the years. The difference after such interactions can be radically liberating.

I learnt how to preach (with a little classroom help) from watching and listening to good preaching. I learnt how to pray by watching and listening to the saints pray. Here I learned about simple child-like faith that knew God, knew His heart and knew how to gain a hearing. The best way to raise a church to be a praying community is by seizing every of opportunity to practice together.

MORE THAN JUST THE PRAYER MEETING

Of course corporate prayer isn't just about a church prayer meeting. It is also about praying in almost context with at least one other person. In that light it's worth remembering that praying in marriages and as families and with friends is also corporate prayer. It is after all, praying together.

Marriage is amongst other things a context for partnership. We do things together, learn together, achieve together and overcome together. Setting up home, learning how to love each other in all respects; sexually, emotionally, practically and spiritually. Yet it is not always the case that spiritual life together flows with ease.

It came as something as a surprise to me at first but it's more common than I thought as I hear of couples who found it initially embarrassing to read the Bible together and pray together when you are not used to it. Praying together is vital. Husbands need to take the lead, initiative and responsibility in this is I think. It is not that the husband is more spiritual or needs to lead it all, far from it. But much more that men who are passive in spiritual matters in the home are a significant blockage to the healthy spiritual development of everyone living in the home. Yet conversely a husband or father taking an active role is hugely releasing to everyone in the family.

We have found over the years that setting realistic rhythms can help. For example on a day off Sue and I will, as a rule, in the middle of the morning read a daily reflection from Spurgeon's *Chequebook of the Bank of Faith* and then pray for people, issues, ourselves, the week ahead, give thanks for the week past and so on. It is quite low key and not always of great length but it is a rhythm that has anchored prayer for us. We then supplement this spontaneously through the week as it seems to fit and flow.

My advice to any married couple is, no matter how short and simple, just to do something as a weekly rhythm and stick to it. Rhythm and helpful traditions are not bad things. Giving thanks for meals together is such an easy place to start. Every New Year's Day we eat a mid-morning brunch and give thanks to God for the past year, entrusting ourselves to Him for the one to come. Simple 'rules of life' can seem to me quite important to develop in this age of quick change and high mobility.

There is something about pregnancy and childbirth that has rich imagery for prayer. The bride and bridegroom image of Christ and His Church is strong. For us as followers of Christ we are pregnant with His promises for His church. In corporate prayer we can nurture these promises, we as His church are pregnant with them, we are parenting a child born of promise.

> *'Before she was in labour*
> *she gave birth;*
> *before her pain came upon her*
> *she delivered a son.*
> *Who has heard such a thing?*
> *Who has seen such things?*
> *Shall a land be born in one day?*
> *Shall a nation be brought forth in one moment?*
> *For as soon as Zion was in labour*
> *she brought forth her children.*
> *Shall I bring to the point of birth and not cause to*
> *bring forth?'*

says the LORD;
'shall I, who cause to bring forth, shut the womb?'
says your God.

ISAIAH 66:7-9

There is rich imagery here for us to take hold of the things God has promised and learn in prayer that gestation period can be different to what we imagine for the birth of God's promises but as with pregnancy when life is there it will come to fruition in due time. Prayer is very much like watching and waiting for that which we know is to be birthed, because God conceives it. For a church to get hold of this and not let God go until he fulfils his promise, is a very powerful dynamic.

Every church or family of churches should be pregnant with promises from God and express and nurture this confinement with corporate prayer until that which is promised is brought to birth in its due time. Pregnancy fills the family with expectancy; it is an electric time of anticipation. Prayer meetings should be filled with recounting to God the promises both in His word and that prophetically we believe He has made to us. Dull duty does not describe the anticipation of new birth. If prayer meetings become full of repetitive prayers and lacklustre atmosphere it is most likely because we have forgotten we are pregnant with God's promises and purposes. New life is born not because we are waiting for it, but because there is life being formed in the womb. Waiting does not create it, waiting anticipates and celebrates what God has made and promised.

RAISING PRAYING CHILDREN

Parents raise their children in spiritual things. However, children can and should learn to be church and part of that is learning how to pray together. Teaching children how to pray and how to hear God from a young age is important. People know God fundamentally through revelation not information. That is why age or mental faculties are not ultimately the defining factor in whether someone can have a saving relationship with God.

Children learn behaviour, values and world view primarily from their parents. Sunday school or a youth group can play a vital role in the spiritual development of a child or young person; a role that truly introduces them to the special influence of the whole family of God. Even if their own family are not believers they can find a spiritual family to help nurture them in the things of God. However, it is the parent's prime responsibility to raise their children in the things of the Lord.

I was deeply impressed by how Jimmi and Emma's family cultivated prayer and specifically thanksgiving through a time of serious illness. I'll let Emma explain what they did:

I first saw the idea to fill a jar with prayers of thankfulness on Facebook and decided we would give it a go. But before I had even written the first one we found out that Jim had cancer. I wondered whether we should still do it. We decided we would and for us it kind of changed from just putting good things that had happened in the week to milestones in Jim's treatment too.

I made sure I only had a small piece of paper and I usually put 2-3 things down. I tried to include normal life stuff like Noah getting gold cards and reading awards at school and Jake's different achievements over the year as well as always finding the positive to write about Jim's progress.

My favourite ones were the days out and short times away we managed as a family, they seemed to mean so much more as Jim was too ill a lot of the time to be with us. When we were going to read them all out at the start of 2018 everyone was really excited. As I had been the one to write them the boys had no idea what they said, although we counted them before reading began and found I had missed some weeks so the boys all wrote some of their own memories from the year which was really lovely. We took it in turns to read and it was amazing to realise all the things we had still managed to do, what we had been through and how we had made it through the year mostly with a positive attitude. You can sometimes lose heart when times are tough but I know God was with us all the way and it helped me to write these things weekly to help reinforce that. We are filling the jar again this year but with a very different story.

We read in Joshua 4:6 "that this may be a sign among you. When your children ask in time to come, 'What do those stones mean to you?'"

When Joshua and Israel crossed the Jordan they gathered stones into a pile to act as a stimulus for coming generations to recall and rely on the goodness and faithfulness of God. Emma's jar of thankfulness is a modern day 'pile of stones'. Eventually the pile of stones must have been quite noticeable on the landscape. Thankfulness is like that – the more we do it the more we see it.

There is no guarantee that simply through us doing the right things our children will know the Lord. Yet it certainly is the case that, if we have instructed and lived out our faith well, they will develop a sincere respect for that faith and we trust that the work of the Holy Spirit will then find good soil for the Gospel to take root in their own hearts. It is tragic when, through bad parenting spiritually, a child's heart becomes like stony ground or weed covered soil that makes gospel impact more difficult. Why make it more difficult than it needs to be?

Things like going to church every week model commitment and devotion to the Lord. Praying around the dinner table demonstrates that God is central to family life. Praying and reading the Bible together and discussing spiritual things models that whatever else has gone on in the day, our anchor, our foundation is the word of God.

I used to read to my son Sam children's versions of biographies of Christian men and women who had done great things for God. We used to watch some programs on TV and if it had content with a moral or spiritual lesson that could be talked through, good or bad, we would discuss it and maybe pray together at bedtime. Worship and music were part of life. Don't get the wrong idea – our family life wasn't one long worship or prayer time. There was more football in the back garden than praying, but the thing was is that prayer was woven into normal life.

We also shouldn't discount children from participating in church prayer meetings. One feature of what I believe is a present and new move of the Holy Spirit concerning corporate prayer in the West is how engaged children and young people have been with prayer. It took me by surprise. Lots of creativity is needed, finding different ways to pray and express prayer. Interestingly often adults quite like doing these also.

If truth be told children can teach adults much about prayer. Jesus illustrated true faith by likening it to the simple trust of a child. Child-like faith is precious. We must take care never to lose that simplicity, to let cynicism, disappointment or complexity quash simple trusting of God. Children teach us that true corporate prayer does not have to be complex or long. Fellowship together with God is not time dependent it is just learning to know when we have fellowshipped with Him, engaged with Him and when He says we are done with that bit of the day and can now move on. Children seem to move effortlessly from prayer to play and back again while adults often seem as if they need to make it feel religious for it to be authentic.

I'll let Jodi share with you how she has helped children engage in corporate prayer at our church in Lowestoft.

I have found that as I've invested more time in prayer personally and grown in my confidence I've found it easier to step out and lead the children and young people in this area and I've also found that they follow easier, rather than me dragging them behind!

We have observed when praying with children and youth in both and school and church setting that our perspectives of their 'issues' have to be kept in check. As adults we can have a tendency to look upon the pray requests of our children and young people as trivial. We see things from our 'grown up' perspective and filter it through our lens forgetting they are just as important to God as our issues are.

In our Sunday morning group for year 7-9 youth we had a session of praying for our 'goliaths', those things in our lives that feel unsurmountable. The session had been great and there had been a crescendo to a response calling the young people to write down their 'goliaths' and place them in our giant outline masking taped on the floor. After a few minutes of the young people scribbling away and laying their prayer points down we stood around our giant to pray together and I began to silently read everything they had written. Within minutes I went from being frustrated at their trivial prayer points to being convicted by the Holy Spirit of my thought patterns. "Who are you to say they are trivial" I felt God ask me, "Do I say that to your prayer point!?" A huge lesson was learned then and there, what seems like a 'David' to me, can be 'Goliath' to someone else and vice versa.

My personal journey of identity, of learning more of who I am and how God sees me has helped me to radically shift my gaze from 'what people say, goes' to 'what He says, goes' and that's a liberating place to be because not only does it free me to see my prayer life as valid when I pray in the way that makes me tick (for me that's writing prayers down) but it gives me permission and confidence to lead others there too. I have found that children and young people are ignited to pray when they realise who they are in Him and that they are built to do it. Some love writing, others dancing, drawing; some painting, others modelling with playdoh; some playing instruments, others talking; some shouting, others singing – when these things help us to communicate with God, they are prayer languages and they are valid and can (and dare I say should) have space in our church lives.

Our experiences of our Enough *prayer events are that our children and youth want to be involved, they are passionate about praying for their friends and our communities. They don't want to be seen as a separate entity to the rest of the church. It is a myth that children and young people don't want to mix with older generations. They love their church family and the bridge between generations is easily built when we just 'do church' together as a family, encouraging our children and youth to bring words and pray in our meetings, speaking directly to them from the front of the service, inviting them to read things out for us, asking them to lead a prayer section.*

Those Enough *events where our children and youth have got involved with leading a section have been my favourite; faith is fuelled when the adult church see our young people passionate about what they believe and about who they are praying for.*

I would encourage the nurturing of spiritual mothers and fathers in Christ. We all need them. Even if you consider yourself to be a mother or father in the faith to others, remember even fathers need fathers and mothers need mothers. I will intentionally cultivate time to visit my fathers in the faith, even stay over to get some unhurried prayer time together.

I have the joy of seeing a number of younger men around me emerge into fruitful callings. I am surrounded by dear friends, co-labourers in the work. One of my joys is to arrange a prayer walk day with a team member or younger brother. We meet up for a breakfast and catch up. I have a very nice river-side walk to an old church not far from my home town. The walk out to the church gives time for establishing what needs prayer. The walk back is spent praying.

Creative ways of praying with couples, older people, younger people, etc. should be a high priority for all leaders. A walk and a pray is often more fruitful than sitting in an office discussing. It is all too easy to let pressing matters push us into discussion rather than prayer. It takes courage, leadership and an awareness of just how powerful prayer is to resist that and priorities prayer even if it means we run out of time to discuss something. Corporate prayer will never leave us poorer for time invested in it.

Praying together takes some planning and investment but this is not to make it a programme of church life. When we turn everything into a programme with a department we specialise and prayer is for everyone. When we turn prayer into a programme we become concerned with efficiency, productivity, effectiveness and we start to measure and quantify. We are the family of God and even though we have important work to attend to in prayer we must never forget that we come as family and behave as family before and with our loving Heavenly Father.

7
EVICTION

CORPORATE PRAYER IS LIKE
SERVING THE DEVIL AN EVICTION NOTICE

*The thief comes only to steal and kill and destroy. I came
that they may have life and have it abundantly.*

JOHN 10:10

Imagine a thief who has broken into your house and is now claiming squatter's rights. The intruder helps himself to the contents of your fridge and then sits on your sofa with his feet up, eating your food and drinking your best wine. He flicks through the channels on your TV and throws the rubbish on the floor. He's not just behaving as if he owns the place, but as if no one owned the place. What arrogance!

We would, rightly, feel outraged at such behaviour if we were the injured party. We would, with some urgency, seek to have such a person served with a legal notice of eviction; to have them removed from where they do not belong and to have them stopped from behaving in a way they have no right to behave, with things they have no right to use.

Such a dynamic exists in the world we live in. The Bible says in Psalm 24:1, "The earth is the Lord's and the fullness thereof." This fundamental principle is restated again in the New Testament in 1 Corinthians 10:26. Yet the Bible also states that something has been stolen, something has been taken by the enemy (the devil and his forces of evil). It is like the earth is a house the Lord owns and it has been broken into and the devil is now exercising squatter's rights.

The whole world lies in the power of the evil one.

1 JOHN 5:19

...and they may come to their senses and escape from the snare of the devil, after being captured by him to do his will.

2 TIMOTHY 2:26

In their case the god of this world has blinded the minds
of the unbelievers, to keep them from seeing the light of
the gospel of the glory of Christ, who is the image of God.

2 CORINTHIANS 4:4

All of the above verses use different images to convey theft, destruction, ruinous deception of people and misuse of things belonging to the Lord. It is as though the devil has a residency in places and amongst people that are not rightfully a realm he should be exercising any authority over. There is no doubt from the scriptures that the devil and his demonic forces are exercising significant control over this world and the people in it.

Ephesians 2:2 says we once walked in sin, "following the course of this world, following the prince of the power of the air, the spirit that is now at work in the sons of disobedience."

We should feel outraged at this squatter who with his cohorts in evil has taken residency in the Lord's property. This outrage should lead us to action.

Prayer engages with the process of taking back and reclaiming for the Lord what is rightfully His. Corporate prayer is like serving a legally enforceable 'notice to vacate' or quit. The Bible is an authoritative document that has legal standing over such affairs. Whenever one of God's promises or principles is stated in prayer it is like serving a weighty document of eviction.

When someone arrives at a house with squatters, it is not the force of the person's voice, personality or bodily strength that ultimately brings about compliance. It is rather the fact that however nervously and sheepishly they deliver it, a legally binding eviction notice has been served. No one and nothing can ultimately withstand such a legal notice. Why? Because a higher authority stands behind the notice of eviction so the trespassers have to go. It is written.

When we pray back to God His promises, we are presenting a legal notice of eviction to the forces of evil infesting the world around us. We are giving them marching orders.

DON'T BE POLITE, PRAY!

I can recall moments when prayers have seemed to tip from polite, carefully worded requests crafted in reverence before a holy God, to blunt, almost rude insistence. At such moments we must ask whether the asker moved into disrespectful sin, or whether something deeper and more holy is going on. I am convinced it is the latter. On a few occasions when we have been praying together, the nature and earnestness of the issue has caused my wife not only to pray more directly and insistently about the matter in hand, but to emphasise the earnest nature of her request she has tapped her finger on the palm of her other hand. This I believe is an example of what the Bible refers to as importunate asking. In each case, as I recall, such prayers were answered. Importunity is the insistent and persistent request that refuses to be denied.

Jesus seemed to encourage such prayer. He told the story of the judge and the widow who refused to be refused. He commended the Canaanite woman who quipped back at Him, when He seemed to ignore her, that even dogs got crumbs from the table! Perhaps our prayer meetings are too polite at times? Perhaps they need to tip into 'finger tapping' moments of insistent request.

John Chrysostom put it like this: "Among human beings, importunate asking, seeking, & knocking are considered rude, 'troublesome & disgusting', but with God, not to come asking eagerly is displeasing."[21]

Importunate does not mean disrespectful, quite the reverse. It is because the asker knows that the one being asked has the power and therefore respects who they are and what they can do that the insistence flows. God is not looking for politeness, He is looking for faith. Faith in who He is, what He alone can do and what He has promised to do.

Some have mistakenly thought passion, volume and an atmosphere of war-like fervour is a pre-requisite to effective prayer. This is incorrect. Fervour, passion and even volume express our emotion about the things we are praying for but are not essential to prayer. A sense of urgency in our tone, voice and posture are all equally in keeping with the seriousness of what we pray for.

---

[21] Chrysostom as quoted in Frederick Dale Bruner, *The Christ Book. Matthew 1-12* (Wm B Eerdmans Publishing Co, 2004), p. 344.

As Spurgeon says, "I would sooner risk the dangers of a tornado of religious excitement than see the air grow stagnant with a dead formality."[22]

At heart, it is simply the authority of scripture – the weight and content of the document itself – that brings about the changes required. God's word cannot ultimately be resisted. Such awareness when we quote and state it in prayer, especially in large numbers, is a mighty force.

THE OWNER WANTS HIS STUFF BACK

The first thing to say is the rightful owner wants 'his stuff' back. "The reason the Son of God appeared was to destroy the works of the devil" (1 John 3:8).

Jesus is intransigent about the influence of evil. He wants what is His back under His rule and reign. It is His. When we pray we are therefore partnering with Christ concerning things that we are agreed on together. This is why praying "in the

---

[22] CH Spurgeon, *Autobiography* (Banner of Truth, 1962), as quoted in Terry Virgo, *The Spirit-Filled Church* (Monarch Books, 2011) p. 69.

name of Jesus" is so significant. It asserts the authority of the one in whose name we are making the request. But it also serves to make known His will in the situation, conveying that we are not praying things that he is not in agreement about.

> *In the days of his flesh, Jesus offered up prayers and supplications, with loud cries and tears, to him who was able to save him from death, and he was heard because of his reverence.*
>
> HEBREWS 5:7

Jesus cares and longs for sin and death to be defeated. He longs for people who are held captive to the blindness that sin brings, to come to a realisation of their need of a saviour. He longs for spiritual renewal and social justice to flow on earth as it is in heaven. It matters to Him. No matter how passionate we feel about some things, Jesus is far more moved in His very core. At times those who pray might find themselves feeling some of the emotion Christ feels as they pray.

I live very near the beach and on occasions I walk the beach praying. The desolate location of this lends itself to feeling free to express with feeling some of my prayer requests. I have on occasions throughout my Christian life found myself sobbing with great, almost overwhelming bodily convulsions, and at times it has unsettled me. I have almost felt I am watching myself and not feeling my own emotion but someone else's. I came to realise at times the Holy Spirit was falling upon me with the manifest presence of God, sharing with me, with his own groans and sighs too deep for words, some of the longings of the heart of Christ.

Romans 8:26 says:

> *Likewise the Spirit helps us in our weakness. For we do not know what to pray for as we ought, but the Spirit himself intercedes for us with groanings too deep for words.*

Often, we stop there – at noting individual experience. As this book is about corporate prayer, I would like to make the point that this very verse is written to a corporate context: "we" do not know how to pray. What if as churches at prayer, great waves of longing and lament and petition should flow over us? I would like to suggest that sometimes waves of Holy Spirit which initiate emotion, expressing the heart of God, can and should rest on and permeate the whole atmosphere of a larger scale prayer meeting.

THE PROCESS OF VICTORY

When we pray "Your kingdom come" we are lining up our requests with the will and rightful claim of Christ into that matter; that it will reflect His kingdom and not that of the devil and his destructive dark activity.

> *For he must reign until he has put all his enemies under his feet.*
>
> 1 CORINTHIANS 15:25

This can appear a confusing verse at first glance, especially when compared to verses such as Hebrews 10:12: "But when Christ had offered for all time a single sacrifice for sins, he sat down at the right hand of God," and Colossians 2:15: "He disarmed the rulers and authorities and put them to open shame, by triumphing over them in him."

Such verses seem to say that the work is done, victory is established and there's nothing more to do. But let's use our image of a house occupied by an intruder or squatter. The house belongs to someone else. That is established and beyond question. However, the process of eviction and removing traces of the intruder is a process. It is enforced not in order to establish ownership but because of ownership. Jesus does reign over all things – they are His inheritance. He has defeated the devil and all his demons. It is precisely because those things are true that we can pray and preach the gospel full of confidence that it will be effective.

Corporate prayer is a partnership with Christ in establishing the outworking of his rightful claim over the earth. When we pray for people to come to Christ – that salvation would visit an individual – we are agreeing that this reign of Christ over that individual should be realised. Corporate prayer combined with faithful sharing of the gospel is the means by which the inheritance of Christ is gathered in and the reign of Christ is established.

One of the hindrances to maintaining commitment to long term corporate prayer is that we often do not see any immediate difference after we have prayed. In fact, sometimes things can apparently get worse. Our expectations are often at odds with what seems to happen. Understanding the hidden, but nonetheless very real, activity going on all around us in the heavenly, unseen realms is very important.

> *And behold, a hand touched me and set me trembling on my hands and knees. And he said to me, "O Daniel, man greatly loved, understand the words that I speak to you, and stand upright, for now I have been sent to you." And when he had spoken this word to me, I stood up trembling. Then he said to me, "Fear not, Daniel, for from the first day that you set your heart to understand and humbled yourself before your God, your words have been heard, and I have come because of your words. The prince of the kingdom of Persia withstood me twenty-one days, but Michael, one of the chief princes, came to help me, for I was left there with the kings of Persia, and came to make you understand what is to happen to your people in the latter days. For the vision is for days yet to come.*

DANIEL 10:10-14

These verses show us that from the first day of prayer something was released in the heavenly realms by way of a coming answer to the prayer. The verses also show us that opposition of significant spiritual proportions had engaged in opposing what was being prayed for. This resulted in unseen battle and conflict. Daniel was completely unaware of this. All he knew was that he was faithfully praying and perhaps wondering "why is nothing happening?"

We are most often completely unaware of what is going on around us. The vital thing to know is that persistence does pay off and that lack of immediate visible change does not mean huge battles are going on and ground is being taken. The larger the request and the more infested with evil the situation we are praying for, so perhaps greater is the battle going on in the heavenly realms.

Certainly, when we pray in large numbers for spiritual awakening and revival in a nation, or we begin to take steps to plant churches in places where there are very few, we must be aware we are stepping into areas where principalities hold sway and often have done for generations. They are not going to accept an eviction notice without contesting it. They have often lived there so long they feel at home and believe it is theirs by right.

Whether our prayers feel powerful or not is quite irrelevant. We must pray in faith, believing the promises of God, believing God is who He says He is and has done what He says He has. But our effectiveness in corporate prayer does not flow from our own eloquence or from any internal authority we naturally have within ourselves or within the context of our church. Rather, our effectiveness in corporate prayer flows from the Holy Spirit taking our sometimes-"mustard-seed" faith and our sometimes-faltering words and breathing fruitfulness over them.

Let's take another example, this time from the book of Acts, after the healing of the lame man. The people around were astounded at the miracle,

> *And when Peter saw it he addressed the people:*
> *"Men of Israel, why do you wonder at this, or why do you stare at us, as though by our own power or piety we have made him walk?"*

ACTS 3:12

An outstanding miracle occurred which, from the verses before, we can see flowed out of a culture and rhythm of regular corporate prayer the early church had prized and built into its very fabric.

This miracle, rather than having its roots in personal power or godliness, had its roots in the Holy Spirit's power flowing into this situation of need. Our corporate prayer built into the culture of our church life creates the atmosphere and environment in which the Holy Spirit finds it much easier to do what he is looking to do. Peter and John are quick to point to the power of God as the authenticating mark of the manifest presence of God.

The authority felt by the apostles lay in their conviction that this authority had been given to them by Jesus.

> *Behold, I have given you authority to tread on serpents and scorpions, and over all the power of the enemy, and nothing shall hurt you.*
>
> LUKE 10:19

We too receive this authority from Christ to represent him as his ambassadors. We make our appeal through and to the shed blood of Christ, this is where the power comes in prayer. We are weak people with wandering minds and ineloquent words, easily distracted, easily falling asleep, easily losing heart, missing the nudge of God to pray. We are the weakest of apprentices, yet we are His chosen and choice vessels. So we pray together in such a way that even in the weakness of our prayer He is glorified.

I am not looking to urge the creation of some kind of corporate prayer SAS; elite special forces that stand head and shoulders above the likes of ordinary people like you and me. These special folks can see supernatural things, can pray eloquent, stronghold-shaking words, these people can move mountains with ease. Instead I'm calling for an army of regulars. An army of ordinary people who stand together, helping each other believe Jesus when He, in effect, says "Listen folks, when you pray things happen".

We do not need vast vocabulary, we simply need to know whose house it is and that the rightful owner has, with all lawful authority, re-staked his claim. Then serve the eviction notice to the squatters who have made themselves far too comfortable for far too long.

8
TREE

CORPORATE PRAYER IS LIKE
UPROOTING A TREE

In 1744 Jonathan Edwards began to take corporate prayer very seriously. He invited all the churches he had connection with to join him at regular set times to pray. They prayed in their different places, for a season about the same things. He explained his thinking a couple of years later in a book with the rather long title: *An Humble Attempt to Promote Explicit Agreement and Visible Union of God's People in Extraordinary Prayer, For the Revival of Religion and the Advancement of Christ's Kingdom on Earth.* Later known more simply as *An Humble Attempt*, Edwards' vision for corporate prayer was picked up with great zeal by William Carey and those working with him to form the Baptist Missionary Society.

We have in recent times made our own "humble attempt" by inviting local churches to join together, in hubs, to pray in different places but at the same time. It's extraordinary prayer in different locations with a sense of occasion. It's explicit agreement as we focus the themes of our prayers around similar things in the different hubs. It's visible union so that although we are in different places across different time zones, we are meeting on the same day at the same time in our time zones, demonstrating our unity by praying for the same things in large numbers – the prayers of many!

EXTRAORDINARY PRAYER

The "extraordinary" part of Edwards' initial prayer meetings was that they were not the regular weekly or routine prayer meetings of the local church, but were arranged with a sense of occasion above and beyond the normal. These were serious and purposeful gatherings in their intention. Edwards and his colleagues originally decided to hold them for seven years to allow them to determine whether or not anything could be seen by way of answers. Edwards knew things can take time in prayer and called for a long-term commitment.

VISIBLE UNION

The churches who responded to Edwards' call made prayer an expression of their gospel unity. I am still convinced that the small beginnings we have seen with our *Enough* prayer meetings have the potential to draw many thousands more into visible union. We have requested churches, where possible, to come together in 'hubs' (perhaps a minimum of two to three churches), with ideally no fewer than 100 people. These hubs become a tangible expression of our visible union, knowing that it is but a part of a greater whole. In some ways technology allows for a greater visible union than ever before with live streaming, Skype and video calls and messages. Even across continents and time-zones we can have a measure of visible union.

EXPLICIT AGREEMENT

The beauty of many churches joining together to pray for commonly held desires in prayer is the genius of the united prayer time. Edwards felt that the agenda for prayer should be fashioned around what God had said He wanted to do: "That which God abundantly makes the subject of his promises,

God's people should abundantly make the subject of their prayers."[23]

Our model is borrowed from Jonathan Edwards but we took our inspiration from Paul. The verse that inspired us was 2 Corinthians 1:11. Paul is writing to the Corinthian church and he is reflecting on the mission that he is engaged in and thinking about the enormity of it and the challenges this presents. He says to the Corinthians:

> *You also must help us in prayer, so that many will give thanks on our behalf for the blessing granted us through the prayers of many.*

It was that last little phrase, "the prayers of many" that caught our attention when we were thinking about corporate prayer. I think it's true to say looking through the New Testament that you can't find many instances where Paul or any of the other New Testament writers refer to the size of the local church being the important thing in being fruitful in mission. Yes, we all want church to be bigger and grow and for more

---

[23] Edwards, *A Call to United Extraordinary Prayer*, p.106

and more people to come to know the Lord, but even a small church can be fruitful in its locality as it grows – there isn't an optimum size for fruitfulness.

It seems to me, reading this verse, that Paul was very mindful that prayer is more effective the more people that are involved with it, because he talks about the "prayers of many" being the thing that actually provokes the answers from heaven for which we can give thanks.

Spurgeon also seemed to notice the power of many people praying together:

> *Somebody said the other day of prayer-meetings, that two or three thousand people had no more power in prayer than two or three. I think that is a grave mistake in many ways … for have you never noticed that when many meet together praying, warmth of desire and glow of earnestness are greatly increased.* [24]

---

[24] C. H. Spurgeon, 'The Special Prayer Meeting' 20 July 1875 www.spurgeon.org/resource-library/sermons/the-special-prayer-meeting#flipbook/

How can we think about how this concert of prayer, this coming together in prayer is more effective because we are many?

Some years ago in our back garden, we had a conifer tree that had grown very large. It came to the point where we had to cut it down. Being the first time I'd ever had to cut a tree down, I just cut it almost to ground level and then began the long, laborious task of digging all of the roots out. That took a long while and a lot of sweat, and I was sure we left some of the roots in. It was the first time I'd ever done it and it wasn't the tidiest job. After finishing, I thought "I don't want to do that again in a hurry!" It was a lot of work to get those roots out – lots of single-handed hard work.

Some years later, this time in our front garden, we had a willow tree which had also become too big for the garden. I remember thinking with some concern that we'd have to go through all that root digging again. A friend, who was more knowledgeable in tree surgery than I was, gave me some advice. He said that when we cut the tree down, rather than cutting it all the way to the ground, cut it down so it was about at head height. His experience was that if we were to do that, then a group of us could get hold of the trunk and lever it out. Together we could uproot it much more easily than we would have done with a spade at the roots.

We followed his advice, and although we still had to do a lot of digging around the base of the tree – it didn't just pop out of the ground – nevertheless, the comparison between levering the trunk with a group of friends, and working on your own digging roots with a spade is stark. The more friends you've got helping you to use the trunk as leverage the easier it is to uproot something.

Now apply that to corporate prayer and I believe the imagery works. Praying on our own is powerful. James tells us that Elijah was a man just like us, and that "the prayer of a righteous person is powerful and effective" (James 5:16-18). So we know one person's prayer can make a huge difference. Yet there is also this emphasis in the Bible that when churches come together, across the generations – whether you are a young Christian, or have been a Christian many years, whether you are a child or a pensioner, whatever age, whatever experience – when we come together and leverage our prayers together in these great concerts of prayer, something incredibly powerful happens that can spiritually uproot things.

The roots are an image of the enemy's infiltration into the world around us. The Bible says that the earth is the Lord's and everything in it. But the devil has come like a thief, a liar, a cheat and a destroyer, and we can see the demonic roots of his work penetrating lots of areas of our world. They penetrate the nations we live in, the communities we live in, and the lives of the people around us that we know and love, as well as big global issues. Sometimes in other parts of the world, the roots of the enemy's work are so devastating you can hardly see any soil. We might think, "How do we uproot all of this?"

But although those roots look impenetrable, the earth belongs to the Lord. These roots should not be there and they need uprooting. When we pray in large numbers (our vision for *Enough* is that it will go to at least 20,000 people across the world), the increased leverage we have means we will begin to see enemy strongholds uprooted. The soil will be freed to be cultivated and to have the seeds of God's kingdom planted.

So as we journey through our concert of prayer together, as we pray about the same things, as we watch the videos, fill in the postcards, do the activities, pray for people to come to know the Lord, every single prayer of every single person is like a mighty leveraging of this great tree trunk. Together we can say: "Let Your kingdom come, let Your will be done, on earth – in the earth even – as it is in heaven". We will be pulling together, lending our spiritual weight to the end of the lever to bring about the will of God as it is in heaven.

Now that doesn't mean that we don't then have to go out and work hard! We still have to share the gospel, to influence communities and be good news to those around us, we still have to do some digging – prayer doesn't replace the work we have to do. Jesus says go into all the world and preach the gospel, so we've got to still do stuff, but it's a whole lot easier to do kingdom work when we have already begun to leverage in prayer the things that we want to see happen, so that when we dig at those roots, they come up a lot easier.

WILL YOU JOIN THE REVOLUTION?

The aim of this little book is to recruit you and your church into a prayer revolution. Across the generations and nations, corporate prayer has ebbed and flowed as God has moved and worked across many peoples.

We face remarkable opportunities to change things in our world both by what we do and say and also more foundationally by our collective prayers.

Through prayer there is no problem that can't be solved, no sickness that can't be healed, no burden that can't be lifted, no storm that can't be weathered, no devastation that can't be relieved, no sorrow that can't be erased, no poverty cycle that can't be broken, no sinner that can't be saved, no perishing that can't be rescued, no fallen that can't be lifted, no hurt that can't be removed, no broken relationship that can't be mended, no difference that can't be resolved, no hindrance that can't be shaken, no limitation that can't be overcome, no mourning that can't be comforted, no ashes that can't become beauty, no heaviness that can't be covered with the garment of praise, no thirst that can't be quenched, no hunger that can't be filled, no dry ground that can't be flooded, no desert that can't blossom, no congregation that can't be revived, no preacher that can't be anointed, no church pews that can't be filled, no church leadership team that can't become 'one', no community that can't be Christianised and no nation that can't be transformed.[25]

If the above is true, and I believe it is, then let us make corporate prayer a "contagion" and continue the revolution. Then we will not only see great fruitfulness around us but it will help bring prayer back onto the front foot of church life, which is where is should be.

---

[25] Anon, adapted by Tony Cauchi from Mary Stewart Relfe, *Cure of all Ills* (League of Prayer, 1988), p. 5 www.revival-library.org/index.php/resources-menu/revival-quotes/prayer

9

APPENDIX: TOOLBOX

SOME PRACTICAL SUGGESTIONS FOR GROWING IN CORPORATE PRAYER

Heaven is my throne, and the earth is my footstool. What kind of house will you build for me? says the Lord. Or where will my resting place be?

ACTS 7:49 (NIV)

And he was teaching them and saying to them, "Is it not written, 'My house shall be called a house of prayer for all the nations'? But you have made it a den of robbers."

MARK 11:17 (ESVUK)

For the LORD has chosen Zion; he has desired it for his dwelling place: "This is my resting-place for ever; here I will dwell, for I have desired it."

PSALM 132:13-14 (ESVUK)

We all choose where to invest or spend our money or how to spend our time. We make choices and by and large those choices are around the things that we value the most, that excite us the most and that interest us the most. Building a house (a house of prayer) is only going to be something we give time, energy and investment to if we value what we are building. We will find we have built a deep relationship with God and a dwelling that takes our breath away. Eileen Crossman wrote of an analogy James Fraser used. Fraser was trying to reach the Lisu tribe in China with the gospel. He said:

> *I feel like a businessman who perceives that a certain line of goods pays better than any other in his store, and who purposes making it his chief investment; who, in fact, sees an inexhaustible supply and an almost unlimited demand for a profitable article and intends to go in for it more than anything else. The DEMAND is the lost state of these tens of thousands of Lisu and Kachin – their ignorance, their superstitions, their sinfulness; their bodies, their minds, their soul; the SUPPLY is the grace of God to meet this need – to be brought down to them by the persevering prayers of a considerable company of*

God's people. All I want to do is, as a kind of middleman,
to bring the supply and the demand together.[26]

Fraser concluded,

I used to think that prayer should have the first place and
teaching the second. I now feel that it would be truer to
give prayer the first, second and third place, and teaching
the fourth.[27]

Building a house of prayer, a church where prayer pervades everything will take time, effort and investment from everyone. Some things are achieved best when done with others. We should pray on our own of course, but praying with others is just as important to our Christian lives. Prayer is like building a big house. One person trying to build it on their own will face a longer wait for the project to be completed than if they had help.

Whether a carpenter or a cardiac surgeon, a plumber or a professor, a young child or a senior citizen, introvert or extrovert, literate or illiterate, academic or more practically

---

[26] Eileen Crossman, *Mountain Rain* (OMF, 2001), p. 181
[27] Ibid., p. 201

minded; whoever you are and however you are wired, building this house of prayer requires you. There is a part of the construction God has assigned and designated for you to be stationed at. Your non-participation might leave a hole in the roof!

Just as bad would be corporate prayer designed and led in only one way in church life i.e. only for a certain kind of worker on the project. This results in the situation where only people wired a certain way fit into corporate prayer; this makes you feel redundant and useless. I am convinced corporate prayer is not for experts, it is for all Christ followers and it should be conducted in such a way that it is an easy fit for us all, with a little bit of application and dedication on our part. Building anything takes effort. Trying to build something you don't feel trained for is frustrating and demotivating.

Prayer does take some training just as any other building trade requires training and skill. However, prayer can be learnt by all of us. Remember Jesus taught His disciples how to pray. They felt they needed some help to do it right. Learning how to use the tools of corporate prayer is like an apprenticeship. It requires that we see the finished product in our minds. We have to use the tools again and again, until we can make what we have seen in our minds. Many of my best prayers and preaches have come about when I have been day dreaming or at night half asleep. I awaken and think "If only I could pray like that when I try to!"

Corporate prayer is co-working with God and His people. He knows what He is building. He has in mind the house's design. We are not working on our own to reach Him, He is working with us on a project together. We must remember it is our willing obedience and not our skill and ability that leads to victory. Even when we find ourselves lacking in the former, His grace and love for us are completely sufficient for our lack. He is big enough to save us from everything that is wrong with us. He takes the pressure; He is the foreman and in charge. He is keener on building the house than we are. He says "My house shall be". It is His not ours.

What then are the tools we need; how do we construct this house of prayer? To put it another way, what does the ideal corporate prayer meeting look like and how does it come together?

FASTING

Fasting used to confuse me. As it is something we do, I questioned, "Does it make my prayers more effective?" It felt like a 'work' – something we do to gain something. It helped me to think of fasting as a weapon to gain ground not a work to gain merit.

I am reminded of the scene in the film *Crocodile Dundee*. When Mick Dundee is confronted by youths who pull a knife, attempting to mug him, Mick looks scornfully at the knife and says, "That's not a knife; *this* is a knife", and pulls out his outback hunter's knife, dwarfing that of his would-be attackers. Fasting is such a knife! There are seasons when prayer combined with fasting is a very appropriate and potent combination. For instance:

> *"As soon as I heard these words I sat down and wept and mourned for days, and I continued fasting and praying before the God of heaven".*
>
> NEHEMIAH 1:4

When he heard of the poor state of Jerusalem and God's people, Nehemiah's heart responded by identifying with how

God must have also been feeling. His prayers in that context mixed rightly and powerfully with a season of fasting ahead of a season of working to restore things.

In recent times I have found a simple Friday lunchtime fast, combined with giving that time to God in prayer where possible, is a sustainable discipline which helps me express various things to God. Fasting helps me determine that I will not be governed by my appetites and that my priority and devotion is to God above all else. Fasting also helps me express my longing for God to move and humbles me as I see afresh that I am fully dependent on God for all things. As Jesus said, "man does not live by bread alone…".

In cultures of comfort, fasting can be difficult but when we open ourselves to learning from the global Church we find that in nations where persecution of the Church is common fasting is an essential tool for building the Church.

WORSHIP

It helps having good musicians serving the meeting. Not necessarily a full band, but just something that enables music to be available as required all through the prayer meeting. My preference is for a worship leader able to pick up known songs started by the church and facilitate both singing in the Spirit (tongues) and collective singing when individuals sing out psalms, hymns and spiritual songs. An experienced leader can flow into songs that are appropriate in the moment that might not have been on the 'set list'.

Worship and thanksgiving should be focused on the nature and character of God – His promises and works on our behalf. Psalm 100:4 says, "Enter his gates with thanksgiving, and his courts with praise! Give thanks to him; bless his name!" Coming before God giving thanks for who He is and what He has done, is a vital context for our prayers. We think about to whom we are speaking, rather than the size or complexity of the issue.

SPIRITUAL GIFTS IN CORPORATE PRAYER

Knowing when to abandon the plan because it seems the Spirit is leading you to something else, and knowing when to bring a Holy Spirit diversion back to what was intended are not easy things to learn or do. As a result I always favour a team leadership of a prayer meeting where two or three can consult on what the next move should be in going with what God is doing.

PROPHECY

Often I find, especially in churches very comfortable with charismatic gifts, a huge tactical mistake is made whereby we hear the subject introduced then try too quickly to hear God. Non-charismatic churches are often better at praying as they don't know what else to do! Present your requests, don't rush on into prophecy. Don't prophesy about it; pray into it!

Having said this, when churches receive genuine prophetic words it is God giving us a large part of the prayer agenda for the church in the season ahead. We must pray his prophetic promises into being, however long this takes. Prophetic words must not be filed and forgotten but used as fuel for ongoing vision and prayer.

GIFT OF TONGUES

The importance of praying with our Spirit as well as our mind is seen in Paul's reflection in 1 Corinthians 14:15: "What am I to do? I will pray with my spirit, but I will pray with my mind also; I will sing praise with my spirit, but I will sing with my mind also". We can often find ourselves tired and lacking mental energy in corporate prayer. What is more I think we in the West should press through so we pray in tongues more than feels comfortable, to the degree that perhaps our logical minds are offended. To those who might say "What about outsiders?" I would say that corporate church gatherings for prayer are aimed at the church. I have written elsewhere on the use of tongues corporately,[28] suffice it to say I do believe it is an important component, either spoken or sung in corporate gathered prayer.

PLANNING

Planning a prayer meeting in a gathered church setting is very important. Planning should aid spontaneity not hinder it. When you have all the tools in the box ready and the plans laid out you can then add in your own design and style to create a bespoke item. Ben Patterson says,

---

[28] www.thinktheology.co.uk/blog/article/tongues_and_more_tips_a_response_to_andrew_wilson

Good corporate prayer in a large group also requires planning, at least as much as would go into any other well planned service of worship. Many prayer meetings fail precisely at this point. For some reason the idea is out there that a prayer meeting should simply 'flow' spontaneously in the Spirit, meaning that there should be no planning, since planning would somehow stifle the flow. [29]

Good planning means having an agenda that guides the meeting. The person leading should keep the meeting moving along and running to time. I have found people are more able to engage in corporate prayer if the agenda moves fast, has lots of creativity in it and is full of stimulation. Clearly there are times when the Spirit of God will brood over a meeting or a part of the agenda and we should then yield to this even if it means some things are carried over until next time, but it's better to have a plan and abandon it than to have no plan at all.

---

[29] Ben Patterson, *Deepening your Conversation with God* (Bethany House Publishers, 1999, 2001), p. 169

ROOM SETUP

I'm just going to throw this one out there: think about how you set up the room and if possible avoid rows. It is difficult enough to pray without trying to pray into the back of someone's head. The church a family coming together not strangers sitting on a bus.

In addition, as space allows, hubs have created prayer stations around their meeting room. These spaces allow for different ways of praying and can make prayer more accessible especially for children.

PRAYER AGENDAS

What to pray for? One area surely to be built strongly is surrounding learning how to pray back to God the things He has promised to do. As observed by Jonathan Edwards, "That which God does abundantly make the subject of his promises God's people should abundantly make the subject of their prayers."[30]

---

[30] Edwards, *A Call to United Extraordinary Prayer*. p. 106

Praying back God's promises covers both the small but important details of our lives ("Give us this day our daily bread") and also lifts our eyes to the vast and global horizons of God's purposes on the earth ("the mountain of the house of the Lord shall be established as the highest of the mountains" (Micah 4:1)).

Building a prayer agenda for a corporate prayer meeting can be aided by looking at the components of the Lord's Prayer and following the flow of this. Worship, thanksgiving, God, His nature and His promises, requests for intervention and guidance, personal collective needs for provision and cleansing, appeal for deliverance from evil etc. Teach people to say in effect when they pray, "Lord, You said…." And use that as the basis upon which we make our requests. This is not only biblical but it protects us from fanciful or spurious emphasis in prayer.

One of the things I recall about church many years ago was the 'minister' praying at some point in the meeting. Usually it included prayer for the nation, for current affairs, for the church, and an appeal to God for him to save, touch and heal those around us in the local community. It carried a dignity about it that I have never forgotten. I would suggest this may be something to recover. There is something about someone leading the church in a gathered collective prayer for the nation or large-scale things. It is one way of outworking the encouragement in Timothy to pray for "kings and all in high positions" remembering it is encouraged "first of all" (1 Timothy 2:1-2) – it should be a feature of the meetings. To those in church settings where spontaneity and lack of formality is treasured, I would make the point that there is nothing wrong with preparing one such prayer, or at least the things you want to include in it and then taking five minutes to lead a congregation in it in an otherwise unstructured meeting.

Another popular feature of our large scale corporate prayer gatherings called *Enough* is the "Prayer Postcards". We select two or three church planting or pioneering situations from amongst our family of churches each term. Across the hubs we watch a short video shot on location which gives everyone a few prayer points for the church plant. We then spend some time praying for that church plant in large numbers. At the end of the prayer time postcards are distributed and time is given for people to write out prayers, verses, prophetic encouragements, etc. for each plant. These postcards are then collected and sent out to the church plant en masse. Children seem to especially like this task. One little boy in our church, George, has appointed himself to be the postcard collector. Anyone not completing a card in the time given receives a stern stare from George!

Don't despise collections of written prayers or praying the creeds. We have tended to move away from that which is perceived as 'traditional' but there is value in some of the practices. Written prayers, collects or creeds can be incredibly helpful tools. Find the impetus again and the practice can find fresh life once more. Have them read out with eloquence by a gifted orator, or projected onto a screen and all read together, then sealed with a resounding, collective "amen". These carefully crafted historical sources have stood the test of time, and can be incredibly powerful. The creeds particularly act as a tremendous plumb-line to the church on truth and error.

After the meeting maybe send a text or e-mail encouraging those who have prayed for the first time or made another helpful contribution.

INVOLVING CHILDREN IN CORPORATE PRAYER

I'm going to let my friends Daniel and Anna Goodman from Cambridge take this one:

We do a lot of talking in church meetings. Talking is a great way to teach and learn... but it isn't the only way. One thing Enough *does is add variety, not only to the way we pray but to the way we learn. Proverbs 22:6 says, "Train up a child in the way he should go; even when he is old he will not depart from it." When we bring our family to* Enough *we show our boys that prayer is important to us. And they see, because there are so many other families there, that it is important to other people too. They haven't learned this because we told them, but because they've experienced it. This is part of training up our children to know for themselves that prayer is a powerful and integral part of our everyday living.*

The visual impact of seeing a map can bring greater comprehension to distances. The physical act of sending an encouraging postcard can itself be encouraging! The contrast between a busy hall full of noise and a quiet space to think can really, well, make you think. The communal dynamic of singing together or eating together can add substance to the idea of 'family'. All these are ways of teaching our kids to pray and live.

Not just our kids, but everyone. Sometimes, as we've moved around the prayer stations, we've seen how other parents engage their kids with the topics, or with tough questions and we've learned something about being a godly mum and dad. Matthew 11:25 says, "Jesus declared, 'I thank you, Father, Lord of heaven and earth, that you have hidden these things from the wise and learned and revealed them to little children.'" Not only are our children learning from us during these prayer times, but we are also learning from them as God reveals things to their hearts. They help to keep us childlike in the way we pray.

ATMOSPHERE

My own aim is that the atmosphere is relaxed and relational not religious and formal. Conversation and refreshments before a prayer meeting I think can help the flow. Informality with reverence is a mighty blend.

Begin the meeting with stories and testimonies about clear and definite answered prayer, of course, but also encourage testimonies about what God is doing in people's lives.

Sometimes we need the help of others to see the connections that we ourselves have missed. Often prayers from some time ago are actually behind what we are seeing God do now. As that happens, celebrate everything you see God do, it builds faith for more, there is huge power in speaking of what God has done. One of my favourite meetings of the whole year is the first Sunday of each year when our meeting in my local church is given over purely and totally to thanksgiving and testimony of what God has done in people's lives through the past year. It is always a stunningly moving and powerful meeting to me!

MOMENTUM

Sometimes though, we just have to pray ourselves into prayer. We don't always get up and think "I can't wait to get to work" but we have to go whether we want to or not. It's the same with prayer; we can pray ourselves into prayer, especially when others are around us, as it kindles something in us all. Like those days you get to work and being with your colleagues just gets you into it. Feelings alone don't build momentum in prayer, it takes effort. The Bible is full of indicatives (the things that are true of us without us doing anything e.g. raised with Christ) and imperatives (the things we are required to do because of who we are e.g. share our faith).

People thrive on encouragement. Don't get boring but instead create an air of expectation: "What will God do tonight in the meeting?" Don't keep talking at the beginning or when introducing the next subject. Keep it short and simple and then get on with it. Some people introduce the subject for so long there are only two minutes left to pray about it.

Don't let people pray out their pet doctrines or their offences. Don't let people hog the prayer time. Don't get into a rut whereby you know who will pray when and about what. It is vital that as with every other kind of contribution corporately people are trained in how to pray helpfully in a gathered context. Especially encourage the validity of repetition and short raw prayers. "God help us", is quite sufficient if that is from the heart and looking to God, placing faith on who He is, not in the eloquence of our requests. If there is life in the meeting, even immature life, then let it get untidy; that is often a sign it is verdant. My garden often needs tidying up. That is a good sign! It means things are growing and it needs managing. A corporate prayer time that is fruitful will require the management of the contributions.

Another often observed error is lack of clear explanation as to what is required of people in the prayer time. Do you want them in groups, how many, where should they stand, what should they pray for, is it 'all together' prayer, how long is it for? Think about and clearly signpost to people what you want them to do. A lack of this is quite often the most observable trait in poorly led prayer gatherings. If you are leading the meeting or a section of the meeting you might know what you want everyone to do, but unless you tell them, they don't!

BE CREATIVE

There's no reason prayer should be boring or done in only one way, so break out of the rut and help your church discover, enjoy and look forward to praying together.

"When God is about to do a mighty new thing He always sets His people praying." Jonathan Edwards

JOIN A GLOBAL CONCERT OF PRAYER FOR REVIVAL

TAKE YOUR CHURCH
ON A PRAYER ADVENTURE

ENOUGH IS:

- A framework for effective and sustained corporate prayer
- Inspiring resources to inform and fuel your prayers
- The opportunity to be part of a unique global concert of prayer

PRAYERSOFMANY.ORG